I0813842

THE BRUNCH CLUB

This book is dedicated to my grandmother – forever the best host I've ever met, always making it look so effortless and glamorous.

THE BRUNCH CLUB

Delicious Recipes and Hosting Tips for Feeding Friends

Georgia Hearn

Contents

WELCOME TO THE BRUNCH CLUB

If there's one thing I've learned through my career as a chef, caterer and serial host, it's that brunch is not just about eggs and bacon. In fact, it's probably the most versatile meal there is.

Brunch can be as casual as an al fresco barbie at home with friends – albeit with colourful and wonderfully tasty salads – or as smart as a multi-course, day-long affair with paired drinks and themed table decorations. The way you brunch is entirely up to you, your mood and the vibe you want to create. If there is one take-away from this book, let it be that.

What I love about brunch is that, unlike breakfast, a traditional Sunday lunch or a more formal-feeling dinner party, there are no rules or expectations to restrict how you do it. Brunch on a beautiful summer's day might be very different from what suits a cold and grey winter's day or, let's face it, the easy comfort you need on a very lazy Sunday after a big night out. While traditionally falling somewhere between 11am and 3pm, there's no reason it can't fulfil the role of a quick and wholesome meal before a day out, while working equally well for a long, drawn-out affair with friends and cocktails.

And who wouldn't want to have two, or even three, of their meals at once? Not only does it make that hosting occasion all the easier, it allows you to make full use of all the different flavours we associate with each meal without any of the barriers. Love chilli with your eggs? Add it on. Fancy a waffle with gochujang? Why not? It's all about finding the flavours you love and experimenting knowing there are absolutely no limits.

While downing a glass of booze for breakfast tends to be rather looked down upon, at brunch it is game on for those that want! Brunch has become synonymous with cocktails over the years as something of an extension of the historical appearance of a mimosa or Buck's Fizz at special occasion tables. However, brunch's diversity means you can pair your meal with a vast array of drinks – from a refreshing rhubarb fizz to indulgent chocolate smoothies!

I hope the recipes I've gathered here not only inspire but also give you a springboard from which to start experimenting and making brunch your own – because this isn't just a recipe book, it's a brunch invitation.

My Brunch Journey

Having grown up in a family of foodies it really came as no surprise to anyone when I announced I wanted to be a chef. All the best memories of my childhood tend to be situated at a dining table eating something delicious surrounded by lots of people and chatter, and this is something I knew I'd want to carry through my life forever and help bring to other people.

I went to train with Leiths School of Food and Wine and the Cookery School at Little Portland Street before starting my own catering company in 2018. Here, I focused on seasonal ingredients and big sharing-style menus, helping my clients to make entertaining at home as easy as possible. To share this mission further I also started posting recipes and hosting tips on Instagram, which has led to some wonderful connections over the years with people who get in touch thanks to our shared ethos.

As a result of my first-hand insight into seeing how entertaining at home has evolved in recent years, I started to notice a real trend for different styles and timings to the traditional night-time dinner party option. With this, I came to see just how perfectly brunch hosting aligned with my mission to support the overwhelmed host with an easier (and hopefully more fun!) way to entertain. This book is the culmination of that journey – a way to inspire others to embrace the joy of hosting brunch and make it their own favourite way to gather, connect and share good food.

How to Use This Book

Recipe key
V = Vegetarian
VE = Vegan

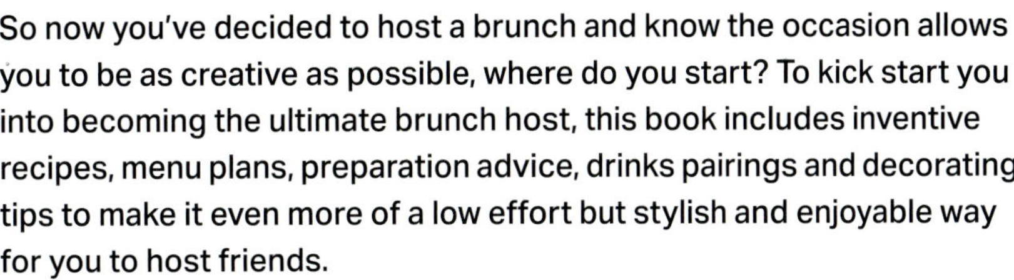

So now you've decided to host a brunch and know the occasion allows you to be as creative as possible, where do you start? To kick start you into becoming the ultimate brunch host, this book includes inventive recipes, menu plans, preparation advice, drinks pairings and decorating tips to make it even more of a low effort but stylish and enjoyable way for you to host friends.

The book is split into different chapters to cover varying occasions and cravings:

Sharing Style contains dishes perfect for combining as small plates to share with others. Feel free to mix and match them all as much as you want – you can even add in some larger plates from the other sections mentioned below!

A Little Bit Special consists of those recipes that require a little bit more time to make, or involve an ingredients list worth investing in. This is the section for when you're cooking for someone extra special, craving indulgence or want to really impress. These are showstopper dishes that wow on their own but still pair perfectly with other dishes across the book.

Lazy Sunday is for when you're nursing a headache or, ideally, looking for a dish that can have you eating said dish as quickly as possible from the bed you've dragged yourself out of. These low-effort recipes are still packed with flavour but come minus the faff.

Something Sweet is possibly my favourite chapter! One of the best things about brunch is the fact you can serve savoury and sweet at the same time, so this chapter had to be filled with very special sweet treats. From crumbles to cinnamon buns and pistachio cake, these are recipes that sing to my sweet tooth and hopefully yours too.

Drinks – because brunch wouldn't be the same without an

extra special beverage. Whether it be the classic brunch mimosa, a healthy green juice or my dad's famous Bloody Mary, the recipes in this section will help bring your whole menu alive.

Sides, Sauces and Extra Bits is where you can find some bonus brunch snacks and sides as well as all the sauces I've used in the book. After all, I've always said that it's the sauces that can take a meal from good to great!

Menu Plans is the chapter that makes it easy to start hosting with confidence. Here, I've put together selections of recipes from across the book that complement each other, complete with drink and decoration suggestions too. Organized by theme, from comfort food to Mexican fiesta, you'll find something to suit every occasion.

Whether it be to replace the Sunday roast, the bottomless celebration version or as a convenient way to feed a family without the early morning wake-up, brunch has arrived and is here to stay.

Time to get started. I wish you lots of fun and good food.

Georgia

Hosting Tips

Thanks to many years of catering experience and being a huge lover of hosting friends and family at home, I've come up with many tips, tricks and helpful practices to make it a lot more enjoyable and stress free.

1. When choosing your menu, pick a theme. This makes it a lot easier when thinking about flavours, time planning and colours. Take into account storage and cooking space too.
2. Stick to recipes you are comfortable with when hosting. It's much better to experiment in smaller numbers, where getting it wrong doesn't really matter.
3. Keep your menu aligned with the current season. Not only does it tend to mean produce is cheaper and much more environmentally friendly, but it's almost always tastier.
4. Sauces make a meal, so always include a couple as they are the best way to make things more exciting, add depth and hide mistakes.
5. Don't be afraid to substitute ingredients to make it work for different diets or to suit the season.
6. Prep as much as possible. Get as many steps of the food preparation done in advance, lay the table and get all the washing up done before guests arrive
7. Write a list of everything you need to do in advance and even time-plan your preparation if you are stressed. This way you can organize timings in advance and simply follow the order at show time.
8. Pretty tables always make things extra special, so invest in a couple of tablecloths, some placemats and candleholders, and keep it fresh and interesting with cheaper props such as candles, flowers and napkin rings. Have fun collecting your own pieces too – I love a good vintage shop for unique tablescape bits.
9. Serve 'help yourself' style. It makes the evening more interactive, takes the stress off plating up and tends to mean there is a lot less food waste on plates if guests can take what they actually want.
10. Always have an empty dishwasher and rubbish bins for when guests arrive.
11. If you are anything like me, you will always err on the side of caution and end up with plenty of leftovers. I like to keep old packaging like glass jars and plastic tubs around so I can send guests home with a very delicious lunch the next day.
12. Most importantly, try to relax and have fun! Your guests are there to see you, and no one will be judging you if everything doesn't go exactly to plan.

Get Ahead

My friends tell me I am a broken record when it comes to suggesting people 'get ahead' but it really is the key to hosting a successful event. In short, spread your to-do list out over a couple of days to keep preparations as stress-free as possible.

1. Design your menu with at least some recipes that can be made ahead of time and simply reheated when needed. Many recipes (including in this book) have make-ahead tips so be sure to make the most of them.
2. Don't be afraid to use the freezer where you can. This will enable you to make things far more ahead of time than simply a couple of days.
3. When designing your menu, choose recipes with overlapping ingredients. Not only is this far more cost-effective and tends to mean recipes pair together better, it's also a great way to save on time as you can prep said ingredients all at once.
4. Remember, baked goods can often be made a day in advance.
5. Even if there is a recipe that doesn't lend itself to resting or being made ahead of time, such as a piece of fish, you can still get all the ingredients measured out and vegetables chopped – mise en place!
6. Get your serving plates out at the ready, and decide which dish will go on each one. You can even write it down or label them. This sounds overly simple but all these small things done ahead of time really make a difference. Include the serving spoons too!
7. If you are serving cocktails, pre-make any fruit juice mixes and store in the fridge until ready to serve. Just hold back on adding the ice and anything fizzy until serving.
8. Keep the menu seasonal – it will mean they are more likely to have it in your supermarket and alleviate any last-minute stress if you forgot something.
9. If you are really nervous about a menu, practise it ahead of time.

A NOTE ON EGGS

Please note that all eggs used in the recipes in this book are large (US extra large) organic.

Recipe Log

Sharing Style

A Little Bit Special

Lazy Sunday

Something Sweet

Drinks

Sides, Sauces and Extra Bits

SHARING STYLE

Over the years I've seen a real rise in people preferring a sharing style format whilst entertaining at home – I myself really only host this way. It means you can have lots of different options to suit all dietary and preference requirements, which is a lot less fiddly than having to make up individual plates. As a bonus, it is also a lot more social and interactive as the guests can serve themselves.

In this section, many of the dishes go well together, but feel free to mix and match from the other sections too. I encourage you to experiment and have fun creating your own combinations. The possibilities are endless!

To make serving multiple dishes at once as stress-free as possible, these recipes come with make-ahead tips wherever relevant, as well as ingredient swaps to accommodate various dietary needs. They're all written to serve four, making it easy to scale up or down depending on your guest list.

Porridge bread, p148
2
Chimichurri, p157

3
1

Slow cooked courgettes, salted yoghurt and zaatar v

Courgettes (zucchini) come with so much summer nostalgia for me, and it's the vegetable I use more than any other during the warmer months. They are so versatile, but slow cooking them is my favourite way to enjoy them and it's something I don't see on people's tables enough. Paired with the yoghurt, this dish is a dip/salad hybrid and lends itself to all sorts of different meal occasions.

SERVES 4

- 6 courgettes (zucchini)
- Olive oil and salt
- 2 tsp of zaatar, plus extra to garnish
- 250g/9oz thick Greek yoghurt
- Lemon zest and honey to garnish

Start by chopping the courgettes (zucchini) into rounds 1cm (½in) thick.

Place in a frying pan with 2 tbsp of olive oil, the zaatar and a big pinch of salt. Place over a medium-high heat.

Stir the courgettes often and cook for 30 minutes until a really deep golden brown and just holding their shape. Once there, remove from the pan and leave to cool to room temperature.

Whilst the courgettes cool, mix together the Greek yoghurt with a pinch of salt. Spread over the base of your serving plate.

Top the yoghurt with the cooked courgettes, grate over the lemon zest, drizzle with some honey, sprinkle with zaatar and you are ready to serve!

Alternatives

Use a dairy-free yoghurt to make this recipe plant-based.

MAKE AHEAD

The courgettes can be cooked a day ahead and stored in the fridge in an airtight container but make sure to let them come to room temperature before serving. The salted yoghurt can be made the day before and refrigerated too, but serve this cold.

② Tomato butter beans, salsa verde and anchovy

Beans are really having their moment and this is my favourite way to enjoy them. In the summer, I like to make this with really good quality, fresh tomatoes but these can be subbed for two tins of chopped tomatoes in the colder months. It pairs especially well with the crunchy potato rosti (see page 151) for a delicious combination of texture and flavour.

SERVES 4

— Olive oil and salt
— 3 garlic cloves, thinly sliced
— 1 tsp caraway seeds
— 1 red chilli, finely chopped
— 2 tbsp tomato purée
— 1kg/2lb of good quality tomatoes, finely diced
— 1 tbsp caster (superfine) sugar
— 1 tbsp red wine vinegar
— 2 jars of butter beans (lima beans), drained
— Salsa verde (see page 157) and anchovies for garnish

Start by placing a large saucepan over a medium heat with a drizzle of olive oil. Add the garlic, caraway seeds and chopped chilli and sauté for a minute stirring continuously till fragrant.

Add the tomato purée and stir together with the garlic mix. Then add the chopped tomatoes with 200ml/7 fl oz/¾ cup water, the sugar, red wine vinegar and a large pinch of salt.

Bring the heat down low and let the mix simmer for 15–20 minutes, stirring often until the tomatoes have broken down and you've got a thick tomato sauce seasoned to your taste.

Stir through the drained butter (lima) beans. Once the beans are warmed through, it's time to serve.

Place the tomato beans in a large serving bowl. Drizzle over the salsa verde, garnish with anchovies and serve up.

Alternatives

Without the anchovies this dish is vegan but if you are craving the saltiness it's also great topped with capers.

MAKE AHEAD

The tomato sauce can be made up to 2 days in advance and stored in an airtight container in the fridge until ready to use. Simply gently warm the sauce to a simmer and skip to step 4.

③ Whipped ricotta with crispy sage and burnt butter V

A sauce, dip or base for endless topping options, this recipe features at every hosting occasion in my house. For an extra special touch, I love to serve with shaved truffle or grilled artichoke hearts.

SERVES 4

- 250g/9oz ricotta
- 1 tbsp olive oil
- Juice of 1 lemon
- 50g/2oz salted butter
- 30g/1oz sage
- Toasted pine nuts and honey to garnish
- Pinch of salt

Alternatives

I recently made this for a client with a plant-based cream cheese and it worked just as well.

Place the ricotta, olive oil, lemon juice and a pinch of salt in a mixing bowl. Whisk together till smooth and creamy.

Place the butter in a frying pan over a medium heat. Once melted and bubbling, add the sage. Once the sage is crisped, remove the pan from the heat.

Put the ricotta into the serving bowl and make a slight dip in the middle. Pour in the butter and sage mix.

Drizzle over the honey and sprinkle some pine nuts. Serve up!

MAKE AHEAD

The ricotta can be made 2 days in advance and stored in the fridge in an airtight container.

My Tips

It's always a big help to know well in advance if any of your guests have dietary needs and requirements. There's nothing worse than realizing, in the final hour, that half of the dishes you are serving are not edible for one of your party!

To help you out, you'll find lots of options for adjusting the recipes in this chapter. I have included suggestions for making them plant-based or vegetarian but, if you are catering to a party of carnivores, feel free to experiment by adding some meat.

5
Dad's Bloody Mary, p134
6

4

(4) Caramelized squash with chive, pistachio and ricotta pesto

Squash is my favourite winter vegetable – sweet, caramelized and crispy, it's the star in this recipe, pairing beautifully with the creamy pesto. It's versatile too: serve it with leftover potatoes and sausage for a hearty brunch hash (6) or add the tahini-dressed broccoli (5) for a vibrant, seasonal spread.

SERVES 4

- 1 butternut squash, deseeded and chopped into 8 wedges
- 1 tbsp dried thyme
- 1 tsp chilli flakes
- Olive oil to drizzle
- Salt and pepper to season
- Crushed toasted hazelnuts and chives to garnish

PESTO
- 20g/¾oz chives
- 2 tbsp olive oil
- 50g/2oz ricotta
- 50g/2oz pistachio kernels
- 1 tbsp grated Parmesan cheese
- Juice of 1 lemon
- 1 crushed garlic clove
- Salt and pepper to season

Preheat the oven to 200°C/400°F and line a baking tray with baking paper.

Lay the squash wedges out on the tray, add the chilli flakes and thyme, generously drizzle with olive oil and season. Mix together with your hands and place in the oven for 30–40 minutes till crispy round the edges and soft in the middle.

Place the pesto ingredients in a food processor and whizz till smooth.

Spoon the pesto over a serving place. Top with the squash wedges. Sprinkle with the crushed hazelnut and chives. Give one last drizzle of olive oil and serve.

MAKE AHEAD
The pesto can be made up to 2 days in advance and stored in the fridge.

Alternatives
Replace the pesto with my Chimichurri sauce (see page 157).

⑤ Grilled broccoli and whipped tahini VE

SERVES 4

— Olive oil
— Salt and pepper to season
— 100g/3½oz tahini paste
— 1 garlic clove
— Juice of 1 lemon
— 400g/14oz long-stemmed broccoli
— Crunchy chilli oil (see page 158)
— Chopped toasted hazelnuts to garnish

Start by placing the broccoli on a baking tray. Drizzle with olive oil and seasoning, mix together with your hands so everything is evenly coated and spread out across the tray.

Place the tahini, garlic, lemon juice, 3 tbsp of cold water and some salt and pepper into a food processor and blitz till a smooth, whipped dressing forms. Season further to taste and add more water if it still needs loosening – you want a double (heavy) cream consistency.

Place the broccoli under the grill for around 8 minutes, flipping halfway through, until charred but still al dente. Remove from the heat and let cool slightly before transferring to your serving plate.

Pour the tahini dressing over the broccoli and drizzle over as much of the crunchy chilli oil as you like/can handle! Finally, garnish with the toasted hazelnuts and serve.

⑥ Sausage and rosemary hash

SERVES 4

— 500g/1lb 2oz new potatoes, chopped into bite-sized pieces
— Olive oil for frying
— 1 onion, finely sliced
— 4 sausages, removed from skins and broken into bite-sized pieces
— 20g/¾oz finely chopped rosemary
— 1 tsp chilli flakes
— Salsa verde (see page 157) to serve

Place the potatoes in a saucepan with just enough water to cover and a pinch of salt. Set over a high heat and bring to the boil. Cook until tender. Drain and set aside.

Set a frying pan over a medium heat with a drizzle of olive oil. Add the onions and fry until soft and translucent.

Add the sausage pieces, rosemary and chilli flakes.
Fry for a couple of minutes before adding the potatoes.

Fry for around 10 minutes till the sausage is golden brown and potatoes are crisp.

Serve hot with salsa verde.

Cheesy jalapeño cornbread, p146
7
Crunchy chilli oil, p158

8
9

⑦ Huevos rancheros V

I'm a huge fan of tacos, so including my go-to Mexican brunch recipe was a must for this book! This recipe works at any time of the day and has become somewhat of a staple Sunday-night supper in my house. It's fresh, protein-rich, packed with flavour and comforting all at the same time, and is something I hope you will turn to again and again.

SERVES 4

— 1 x 400g/14oz tin of black beans, drained
— 350g/12oz good quality cherry tomatoes, halved
— Juice of 2 limes
— Pinch of salt
— Vegetable oil for frying
— 4 tortilla wraps
— 4 eggs
— 150g/5oz feta, crumbled
— 2 avocados, finely sliced
— Crunchy chilli oil (see page 158) and chopped coriander (cilantro) to garnish

Start by placing the black beans, halved tomatoes, lime juice and big pinch of salt in a bowl and mix together.

Next, place a frying pan over a medium-high heat with a drizzle of vegetable oil. Add the tortilla wraps, one at a time, and toast for a minute each side till golden brown and crisp. Remove from the pan and set aside.

Place the toasted tortillas on your serving plates and top with a couple of heaped tablespoons of the black bean mix.

Crack the eggs into the oiled pan and fry to your liking. Once cooked, transfer straight on top of the tortilla and beans.

Top the fried egg with crumbled feta, sliced avocado, some chopped coriander (cilantro) and a drizzle of crunchy chilli oil.

Fried eggs, miso dressing and charred corn salad V

I devised this Mexican and Japanese fusion recipe for a brand a few years ago and have been making it ever since. It's crunchy, fresh and colourful, which makes it a wonderful recipe to have amongst a small plate table. Trust me, once you've tried this dressing you will be fully addicted.

SERVES 4

— Vegetable oil for frying
— 300g/10½oz tin sweetcorn, drained
— 300g/10½oz jarred chargrilled peppers, finely chopped
— 2 avocados, finely diced
— 50g/2oz finely chopped coriander (cilantro)
— 2 packs spring onions (scallions), finely chopped
— 100g/3½oz mixed seeds
— 4 eggs
— Tortilla chips to scoop (optional)

DRESSING
— 4 tbsp white miso paste
— 2 tbsp date syrup or honey
— 2 tbsp mirin
— 2 tbsp sesame oil
— Juice of 2 limes

Start by placing a frying pan over a high heat with a drizzle of vegetable oil. Add the sweetcorn and toast for 10–15 minutes till charred.

Whilst the corn cooks, make the dressing by placing all the ingredients in a food processor and blitzing until smooth.

Once the corn is cooked, remove from the pan and set aside to cool slightly before placing in a serving bowl with the peppers, avocado, coriander (cilantro), spring onions (scallions) and seeds.

Add the dressing and mix it all together.

Add a little more oil to the pan and fry the eggs.

Place the tortilla chips, if using, around the edges of the bowl, top with the fried eggs, garnish with more seeds and serve.

Alternatives

Swap the fried eggs for roasted aubergine (eggplant) to make this vegan.

MAKE AHEAD

The corn salad (without dressing) can be stored in an airtight container in the fridge for up to 2 days, and the dressing can be similarly stored in a jar.

⑨ Trout ceviche and crispy rice

While salmon is so strongly associated with brunch, I've opted for a trout recipe, which has similar flavours, appearance and texture but is a far more environmentally friendly option, as salmon has sadly become so over-farmed. You really can't tell the difference!

SERVES 4

— 300g/10½oz cooked hot sushi rice
— 1 tbsp sesame seeds
— 3 tbps sushi rice seasoning
— 350g/12oz sushi grade trout
— Juice of 2 lemons
— 30g/1oz chopped chives
— 2 tbsp soy sauce
— 2 tbsp sesame oil
— 2 tsp hot sauce
— Salt and pepper to season
— Rapeseed (canola) oil for frying
— Chilli slices for garnish

Start by placing the hot sushi rice in a bowl and mixing together with the sesame seeds and sushi rice seasoning. Leave to one side.

Chop the trout into 0.5cm (¼ in) chunks. Place in a bowl and add the lemon, chopped chives, soy sauce, sesame oil and hot sauce, and season with salt and pepper. Mix it all together, cover and leave to one side.

Set a large frying pan over a high heat and generously drizzle with rapeseed (canola) oil.

Whilst the oil heats up, divide the rice into four portions. Roll each chunk of rice into a golf ball shape and then squash into a burger patty shape.

Carefully add the patties to the hot pan and fry for at least 10 minutes before flipping. Flip too soon and they will fall apart, so make sure you can see the edges of the patty crisp and brown first. Once there, flip the patties delicately and cook for around 5 minutes on the other side.

Place the crispy rice patties onto your plate, top with the trout mix and garnish with a chilli slice. Serve immediately!

My Tips

If you are having a lot of people over, why not enlist your friends and family in some preparatory tasks?

Alongside a couple of drinks and snacks, prepping can provide you with the perfect opportunity to spend some more valuable time with your loved ones – even if you are chopping vegetables!

As well as being a lot of fun, it is also a great way to take a job or two off of your plate. Especially if you have someone creative who can get stuck into decorating the table or arranging some freshly cut flowers while you're cooking.

12
10

11
Crispy
smashed
potatoes,
p150
Herby
avocado
sauce, p159

Chorizo, labneh and greens

This chorizo dish is perfect for when you are craving big, punchy flavour – salty, spicy and packed with depth, it's the perfect meaty contrast on a small plates menu. I love serving it alongside some irresistably creamy Turkish eggs (11) and a fresh, spring-focused green salad (12) to bring brightness and crunch. Together, they balance each other beautifully and provide variety in texture, colour and flavour to the table.

SERVES 4

— 4 good-quality chorizo sausages, halved lengthways
— 300g/10½oz labneh or salted thick Greek yoghurt
— Juice of 1 lemon
— 30g/1oz butter
— 2 garlic cloves, crushed
— 800g/1lb 12oz spring greens, hard ends removed
— Pinch of salt
— Chopped toasted hazelnuts
— Lemon zest and chives to garnish

Alternatives

To make this vegetarian, replace the chorizo with paprika-roasted chickpeas (garbanzo beans). Drain a can of chickpeas and place on a roasting tray with 2 tsp of smoked paprika, a drizzle of olive oil and a little seasoning. Mix together, spread out over the tray and roast for 30 minutes at 200°C/400°F until crispy. Serve cooled.

Start by preheating your oven to 200°C/400°F. Place the sausages on a baking tray and cook in the oven for around 20 minutes or until crispy and sizzling. Remove and set aside.

Whilst the chorizo cooks, mix together the yoghurt or labneh, lemon juice and a pinch of salt in a mixing bowl to make the seasoned labneh and leave to one side.

Place a frying pan over a medium heat and add the butter. Once melted and bubbling, add the garlic. Stir continuously and, once fragrant, add the greens.

Stir the greens continuously and cook for around 3 minutes until wilted but still al dente and vibrant green. Remove from the heat.

Spread the labneh mix over the base of your serving plate. Top with the greens and then the hot chorizo.

Garnish with the hazelnuts, chives and lemon zest and serve.

(11) Turkish eggs with chilli yoghurt V

SERVES 4

— 350g/12oz Greek yoghurt
— 2 garlic cloves, grated
— Juice of 1 lemon
— Pinch of salt
— 4 eggs
— Crunchy chilli oil (see page 158)
— Chopped chives, pul biber flakes and toasted hazelnuts to garnish

Place a pan of salted water over a medium-high heat and bring to the boil.

While the water heats, put the Greek yoghurt, grated garlic, lemon juice and a pinch of salt in a bowl and mix together.

Poach your eggs (see page 156 for my perfectly poached eggs) and use a slotted spoon to transfer to a plate lined with kitchen paper to remove any excess water.

Spread the garlic yoghurt out over the base of your serving plate and top with the poached eggs. Drizzle over the chilli oil, garnish with chives, pul biber flakes and toasted hazelnuts. Serve up!

(12) Asparagus, broad bean and herb salad

SERVES 4

— 200g/7oz frozen broad beans
— 300g/10½oz asparagus, woody ends removed and chopped into 2cm/1in pieces
— 200g/7oz frozen petit pois
— 50g/2oz of fresh mint and basil, finely chopped
— 50g/2oz Parmesan shavings

DRESSING
— Juice of 2 lemons
— 3 tbsp olive oil
— 1 tbsp Dijon mustard
— Salt and pepper to season

Bring a pan of salted water to the boil. Whilst you wait, mix all the dressing ingredients in a bowl and season to taste.

Add the broad beans to the boiling water and cook for 2 minutes before adding the asparagus. Cook for a further 2 minutes, and then add the peas and cook for a further 2 minutes, before draining all the vegetables and blanching in cold water so they stay al dente and vibrant green.

Place the drained vegetables in your serving bowl and add the chopped herbs, Parmesan shavings and dressing. Mix everything together and serve.

Salsa verde,
p157
15
13

Grapefruit and rosemary Moscow Mule, p138
14

13 Roasted asparagus, crispy beans and romesco V

Asparagus is my favourite vegetable of all time, so when it's very briefly in season here in the UK during the spring, I try to eat as much as possible. I developed this recipe when trying to come up with fun ways to serve it so my clients didn't get sick of me making it all the time, and it turned out to be my favourite way to enjoy it yet. The crispy beans are addictive!

SERVES 4

- 1 x 400g/14oz tin cannellini (white kidney) beans, drained, rinsed and pat dried
- 450g/16oz asparagus, woody ends removed
- Olive oil to drizzle
- Salt to season
- Salsa verde (see page 157)

ROMESCO SAUCE

- 1 x 350g/12oz jar red peppers, drained
- 150g/5oz toasted flaked almonds
- 3 tbsp olive oil
- 1½ tbsp red wine vinegar
- 2 tbsp honey/agave
- 1 garlic clove
- Salt and pepper to season

Line two baking trays with baking paper and heat the oven to 200°C/400°F.

Place the drained beans on one of the trays with a drizzle of olive oil and salt. Mix together with your hands and place in the oven for 30 minutes or till crispy and golden brown, flipping around half way through.

Place the asparagus on the other tray, drizzle with olive oil and salt and mix together. Put in the oven and let roast for 10–12 minutes until cooked al dente but still vibrant green.

Whilst they cook, blitz together all the romesco ingredients until smooth.

Once the beans and asparagus are cooked and cooled, it's time to plate up. Smear the romesco over the serving plate, top with asparagus spears and the scatter over the crispy beans. Finally spoon over the salsa verde and serve up!

MAKE AHEAD

Make the romesco up to 2 days in advance and store in a jar in the fridge. The crispy beans can also be made in advance and stored in an airtight container in a cool dry place.

(14) Honey and sesame halloumi with beetroot yoghurt V

Honey-glazed halloumi is my go-to when cooking a vegetarian meal. The salty, crispy cheese with the sweetness from the honey is absolutely delicious and it's even better paired with this swirled pink dip. Sweet, earthy, salty, creamy and incredibly pretty, it's also delicious bulked up as a main meal with quinoa or pearl barley.

SERVES 4

— 4 beetroot, cooked and peeled
— 2 tbsp olive oil
— Couple of pinches of salt
— 150g/5oz Greek yoghurt
— Juice of 1 lemon
— 1 garlic clove, crushed
— 2 blocks of halloumi, chopped into slices 1cm/½in thick
— 2 tbsp honey
— 1 tbsp sesame seeds
— 1 tsp zaatar and sprinkle of chopped coriander (cilantro) to garnish
— Salt and pepper to season

Place the beetroot, olive oil and a pinch of salt in a food processor and blitz to a smooth paste. Season to taste and leave to one side.

Next, place the Greek yoghurt, lemon juice, garlic and a pinch of salt in a bowl and mix together.

Place a griddle pan over a medium-high heat. Add the halloumi and fry for 2–3 minutes each side till golden brown and crispy. Once there, remove from the heat and add the honey and sesame seeds. Mix everything together in a bowl so the halloumi is coated evenly.

Add the beetroot purée to the yoghurt and gently stir so you get a ripple effect. Transfer to your serving plate and top with the honey halloumi.

Garnish with chopped coriander (cilantro) and zaatar. Serve immediately!

MAKE AHEAD

The beetroot can be puréed in advance but I suggest mixing with the yoghurt just before serving.

Alternatives

Swap out the halloumi for firm tofu cut into 1cm/½in wide slices to make this dish plant-based, adding oil to the pan when frying.

(15) Burrata, prosciutto and charred peach

The ultimate summer recipe! With the creamy burrata, salty prosciutto and caramelized peach, this recipe has all the sweet and salty flavours I think work perfectly at brunch – the time of the day where every flavour is welcomed and makes sense, just like this salad.

SERVES 4

- — Rapeseed (canola) oil for frying
- — 6 slices Parma ham
- — 3 peaches or nectarines, halved and stones removed
- — 1 burrata ball, torn into pieces
- — 30g/1oz toasted hazelnuts, chopped
- — 30g/1oz basil leaves
- — Drizzle of olive oil
- — Pinch of sea salt

Alternatives

Sub the burrata for spoonfuls of cottage cheese to make this recipe super high-protein, and replace the crispy ham with a plant-based version to make the dish vegetarian.

Start by preheating the oven to 200°C/400°F. Lay the Parma ham slices out flat on a baking tray and place in the oven for around 15 minutes till crispy. Leave to cool and split into shards when cold.

Set a frying pan over a high heat with a drizzle of rapeseed (canola) oil. Place the peach halves flesh side down and let them char. Once lightly toasted and starting to soften, remove from the heat.

Time to plate up. Place the nectarines flesh side up on your serving place and spoon over the burrata. Sprinkle with the toasted hazelnuts and Parma ham shards. Finally, drizzle with good-quality olive oil, tear over the fresh basil and season with flaky sea salt.

MAKE AHEAD

The peaches can be grilled up to 2 days ahead of time and stored in the fridge in an airtight container.

My Tips

As a general guide to creating the perfect sharing menu, I suggest looking for complementary flavours or a crossover in ingredients which will not only make the dishes easier to prepare but will also make your menu feel cohesive.

You can have a lot of fun with picking your favourite seasonal vegetable (or fruit!) and designing a menu based around this. Often, my best dishes come from this kind of seasonal experimentation.

A LITTLE BIT SPECIAL

The showstoppers! Whether it be a recipe that takes a little bit longer, a focus on investment ingredients, or simply a dish that is a real vision once finished, this 'a little bit special' part of the book was a must. At a time when we are often cooking in a rush and looking for speed and minimal ingredients, I think it's sometimes lovely to take a minute to dedicate more time to a recipe and make the finished product a real labour of love.

All the recipes in this section are designed to stand out and don't necessarily need to be served with other dishes alongside. That said, if you do want to make the recipes part of a bigger menu, take some inspiration from my menu plans at the end of the book or add any of the sharing-style plates you feel match well with the meal you are designing.

Pulled pork, hash browns and pineapple salsa

I don't think there is any dish that feels more like a labour of love than slow-cooked pulled pork. This recipe is a real fusion with Mexican flavours and the trusty English hash brown all presented in the style of the French eggs Benedict.

SERVES 6

— 1kg/2lb pork shoulder, boned
— 1 tsp smoked paprika
— 200ml/7 fl oz/¾ cup cider
— 140g/5oz pineapple
— 30g/1oz coriander (cilantro)
— Chilli flakes to your taste
— 150g/5oz good-quality BBQ sauce
— 2 Maris Piper potatoes
— ½ brown onion, finely sliced
— 1 egg
— Vegetable oil for frying
— 6 tbsp sour cream
— Few pinches of salt

Alternatives

Replace the pork with jackfruit to make this dish vegetarian.

Heat the oven to 140°C/280°F and place your pork in the middle of a large roasting tin.

Rub the pork with the paprika and a little salt. Pour the cider over the bottom of the pan, tightly wrap the top of the tin with foil and roast for 4 hours.

Whilst the pork cooks, make the pineapple salsa. Chop the pineapple into 1cm/½in chunks and finely chop the coriander (cilantro). Place both in a bowl with the chilli flakes and mix together. Store in the fridge till ready to use.

Once the meat is done, remove the foil and cover the pork shoulder with the BBQ sauce. Cook for a further 20 minutes until nicely charred.

Whilst the pork chars, make the hash browns. Grate the potatoes into a bowl with the finely sliced onion, egg and a pinch of salt and mix together.

Heat a frying pan with a generous drizzle of vegetable oil. Divide the hash brown mix into six golf ball-sized portions and, once the oil is really hot, place them two at a time into your pan and flatten them. Flip once browned and crispy – about 2 minutes each side. Remove to a warm plate.

Repeat with the other portions until all six are cooked. Transfer to serving plates.

Remove the pork from the oven and use two forks to shred the tender meat into big chunks.

Time to plate up! Top each hash brown with a tablespoon of sour cream, some pulled pork and pineapple salsa, and it's ready to serve.

MAKE AHEAD
The pineapple salsa can be made 24 hours in advance and stored covered in the fridge. As long as you haven't yet shredded it, the pork can be reheated covered in foil for 15 minutes at 200°C/400°F and then a further 5 minutes uncovered, and the rostis reheated in a 200°C/400°F oven for 10 minutes until crisp.

Dutch baby with smoked mackerel, crème fraiche, lemon and dill

I firmly believe Yorkshire puddings should be served with every type of roast dinner and this recipe takes my love of them even further by proving they're perfect for brunch too. Similar to a savoury crêpe but the puffed-up 3D version that brings plenty of wow factor when serving. Play around with the fillings – the opportunities are endless.

SERVES 4

— 6 eggs
— 250ml/8½ fl oz/1 cup milk
— 200g/7oz plain (all-purpose) flour
— 60g/2oz melted butter
— Couple of pinches of salt
— 150ml/5 fl oz crème fraiche
— Juice of 2 lemons
— 240g/8½oz smoked mackerel
— broken into flakes
— Black pepper to season
— 30g/1oz dill, stems removed and roughly chopped

Preheat your oven to 220°C/430°F and place two small pie dishes in to heat.

Put the eggs, milk, flour, half the melted butter and a pinch of salt in a bowl. Use an electric whisk to combine till you have a smooth batter. Leave to stand for 10 minutes.

Whilst the batter stands, place the crème fraiche, lemon juice and a pinch of salt in a mixing bowl. Beat together and leave to one side.

Remove the hot dishes from the oven and divide the remaining butter between both.

Add the batter, put back in the oven and cook for 15–20 minutes until puffed and golden brown.

Fill each Dutch baby with the lemon crème fraiche and mackerel fillets. Season with lots of black pepper and garnish with the chopped dill.

Serve straight away, one Dutch baby between two people.

Alternatives

Keep it to just vegetables for vegetarians or add meat for a more carnivorous option – I love it with ricotta, ham hock and pesto.

Caramelized onion and serrano tortilla

A couple of summers ago I was lucky enough to be cooked a proper tortilla in rural Spain by a local man famous for his recipe, and I've thought about it every day since. It was salty and gooey all at the same time and so different to the tougher version I'd always tried before. Thankfully, he showed me exactly how to make it and I can't wait for you to try it at home yourselves.

SERVES 4

— 250g/9oz Maris Piper potatoes, peeled
— 4 eggs
— Salt and black pepper
— 150g/5oz serrano ham, cut into bite-sized pieces
— Olive oil for frying
— 1 onion, finely sliced
— Fresh herbs of choice to garnish

Start by thinly slicing the potatoes using a mandolin if you have one. Pat the slices dry.

Whisk the eggs with some black pepper and salt in a mixing bowl. Add the chopped serrano ham and leave to one side.

Drizzle a frying pan with olive oil and place over a low heat. Add the onion and potato and sauté for around 20 minutes, stirring often until the onion is caramelized and potato softened but holding shape.

Add the onion-potato mix to the egg bowl and stir together.

Drizzle the pan with some more olive oil then add the potato egg mix. Let cook for 15 minutes on low heat before using a plate to flip and cook the other side for a further 5 minutes. You want the centre to still be a little gooey but the outside golden brown and almost crispy.

Transfer to a serving plate, season and garnish with fresh herbs.

Green juice, p142

Savoury spinach dosa with masala potatoes V

This dosa is my ultimate Indian brunch dish. The addition of spinach to the pancake batter makes it a real eye-catcher while packing it with antioxidants. For other fillings, you could try tomato, burrata and pesto or honey-fried halloumi and tomato salsa.

SERVES 4

— 500g/1lb 2oz Maris Piper potatoes, peeled and cut into 1cm/½in chunks
— Sunflower oil for frying
— 1 tsp mustard seeds
— 1 small onion, finely chopped
— 1–2 green chillies, finely chopped
— 1 tsp ground coriander (cilantro)
— ½ tsp turmeric
— 1 tsp ground cumin
— Juice of 2 lemons
— 60g/2oz spinach
— 1 egg
— 120g/4oz plain (all-purpose) flour
— 250ml/8 fl oz/1 cup milk
— Pinch of salt

To make the masala potatoes, place a pan of salted water on the hob and bring to the boil. Add the potatoes and cook for 10 minutes or until they are cooked through. Remove from the heat, drain and leave to air dry in the colander.

Set a frying pan over a medium heat with a little sunflower oil. Add the mustard seeds and once they start to pop add the chopped onion and chilli.

Sauté for a couple of minutes before adding the potatoes and a pinch of salt and mixing together. Then add the coriander (cilantro), turmeric and cumin and gently stir-fry until the potatoes are coated in the spice mix.

Next, mix through the lemon juice, remove from the heat and leave to one side.

Now it's time to make the dosas. Place the spinach, egg, flour, milk and a pinch of salt into a blender and blitz till you have a really smooth batter.

Place a frying pan over a medium-high heat and drizzle with a little more oil. Once the pan and oil are piping hot, add a thin layer of batter to the pan. Cook for around 2 minutes each side until crisping round the edges and golden brown. Remove to a warm plate and repeat three more times with the rest of the batter to make four dosas in total.

Remove from heat and fill with the warm masala potato mix, fold up and serve.

Crab panzanella

This famous Italian salad, best made with really top-quality ingredients and plenty of big croutons to soak up all the juices, is made extra special when topped with crab. The original recipe was created as a way to use up leftover stale bread to save money, so I love the idea of serving it in totally the opposite way to its original purpose with the addition of luxury crab.

SERVES 4

— 500g/1lb 2oz leftover stale bread, ideally sourdough, chopped into bite-sized chunks
— 1 tbsp dried oregano
— Olive oil to drizzle
— Salt to season
— 300g/10½oz good quality cherry tomatoes, chopped in half
— 600g/1lb 5oz white crab meat
— 1 cucumber, finely diced
— ½ red onion, finely sliced
— 300g/10½oz cannellini (white kidney) beans, drained and rinsed
— 30g/1oz fresh torn basil

DRESSING
— 3 tbsp sherry or red wine vinegar
— 3 tbsp olive oil
— Juice of half a lemon
— 1 tbsp Dijon mustard
— 1 tbsp honey

Start by placing the bread on a baking tray. Add the oregano, drizzle generously with olive oil and season with salt. Mix together with your hands and spread out over the tray. Place under the grill for 5 minutes, flipping halfway and making sure they don't burn, until crispy and golden brown. Leave to one side to cool.

Place the tomatoes, cucumber, red onion, cannellini (white kidney) beans and a pinch of salt in a mixing bowl. Mix together gently.

In a separate bowl, mix together all of the dressing ingredients until emulsified.

Add the crab, croutons, half the basil and dressing to the tomato bowl and gently mix together.

Decant the panzanella to your serving plate, season with fresh black pepper and garnish with the remaining basil. Serve immediately.

Bellini,
p140

Gan Gan's egg mousse with brioche

Gan Gan, aka my grandmother, is the woman who really encouraged my love of food and I learnt so much from watching her cook for large parties, always remaining calm. Egg mousse was a go-to hosting recipe for her that I particularly enjoyed when I visited as it was absolutely delicious. While she served it more vintage style, set in a bundt tin, I've made it a little more modern, but just how she taught me!

SERVES 4

— 150ml/5 fl oz/generous ½ cup hot chicken stock
— 2 sheets gelatine
— 4 eggs, hard-boiled
— 300ml/10 fl oz/1¼ cup double (heavy) cream
— 1 tbsp Worcestershire sauce
— 2 tsps Dijon mustard
— 30g/1oz chives, chopped, plus extra to garnish
— Salt and pepper to season
— Mini peeled prawns (shrimp), toasted brioche and lemon wedges to serve

In a bowl, mix the hot chicken stock and gelatine sheets. Stir until the sheets have dissolved and leave to one side to cool.

Line the inside of individual moulds or a larger bundt tin with cling film (plastic wrap).

Peel the eggs, finely chop and place in a large mixing bowl.

Add the cooled gelatine stock, double (heavy) cream, Worcestershire sauce, Dijon mustard, chopped chives and plenty of seasoning. Mix together and season further to taste.

Pour into your lined mould or moulds, cover with cling film and place in the fridge. Let set overnight or for at least 4 hours.

When ready to serve, remove from the moulds on to your serving plate and gently peel off the cling film.

Serve alongside some prawns, toasted brioche, lemon wedges and extra chives to garnish.

Harissa beef empanadas

The South American equivalent of a Cornish pasty with the addition of Middle Eastern harissa paste to add extra warmth and spice. These empanadas are delicious and actually super-easy to make with the cheat's trick of using premade shortcrust pastry.

MAKES 12

— Rapeseed (canola) oil for frying
— 250g/9oz minced (ground) beef
— 1 red pepper, finely diced
— 1 red onion, finely chopped
— 1 garlic clove, crushed
— 2 tsp smoked paprika
— 1 tsp ground cumin
— ½ tsp ground cinnamon
— 25g/1oz tomato purée
— 1½ tbsp harissa paste
— 1 pre-rolled shortcrust pastry sheet
— 1 egg, beaten
— Salt and pepper to season
— Chimichurri (see page 157) to serve

Start by making your filling. Place a frying pan over a high heat with a drizzle of rapeseed (canola) oil. Add the beef and fry for around 10 minutes till caramelized.

Bring the heat down to medium and add the chopped pepper and onion. Sauté, stirring often, until the veg is softened.

Next add the garlic, stirring continuously. Cook for a minute until the garlic is fragrant before adding the paprika, cumin, cinnamon, tomato purée and harissa paste. Cook for 5–10 minutes till the herbs are cooked and everything is mixed together. Season to taste then remove from the heat and leave to completely cool.

Once the filling mixture is cooled, line a baking tray with baking paper and preheat the oven to 180°C/350°F. Roll out the pastry sheet and use a cookie cutter to cut out as many disks as possible.

Place a teaspoon of mixture into the centre of each pastry disk, wet the rim, pinch both sides together and use a fork to create a crimp effect on the edges.

Place the empanadas on the lined baking tray and brush with the beaten egg before baking in the oven for 20 minutes or until the pastry is golden brown and crispy.

Serve hot or warm with chimichurri for dipping.

Posh ham, egg and chips

Inspired by the English school food classic but made a whole lot more delicious (see page 62). The gooey yolks with the salty ham and crunchy potatoes make for the perfect plate and hopefully comes with a generous dose of nostalgia. The only real trick here is to serve it with really good-quality, thick slices of ham.

SERVES 4

- 4 medium-sized Maris Piper potatoes
- Drizzle of olive oil
- Salt to season
- Drizzle of vegetable oil
- 4 eggs
- 200g/7oz pulled ham hock or 4 thick slices of good quality ham
- Crunchy chilli oil (see page 158)

Preheat your oven to 200°C/400°F.

Fill a medium-sized saucepan with water, add a pinch of salt and bring to a boil. Add the potatoes and cook for 10–15 minutes or until tender. Drain.

Place the boiled potatoes on a lined baking sheet. Use an old jam jar to push down each potato until they are about 1cm/½in thick. Drizzle with olive oil and a sprinkle of salt, and roast for around 30 minutes till really crispy and golden brown. Let rest for 5 minutes.

While the potatoes rest, fry your eggs. Place a frying pan over a medium-high heat with a drizzle of vegetable oil. Crack in your eggs and fry for around 2 minutes until the edges are crispy but the yolk is still runny.

Place a potato on each serving plate and top with a quarter of the ham hock or a slice of ham. Top with the fried egg and a drizzle of chilli oil. Serve immediately.

Folded eggs with truffle v

Scrambled eggs but extra special! It has all the comfort food feels, but made a little more pretty on the eye thanks to the beautiful ribbon effect you get from the folded egg cooking method. Absolutely delicious on its own, but the addition of earthy shaved truffle makes this the ultimate special-but-speedy brunch option.

SERVES 2

— 5 eggs
— Pinch of salt
— 30g/1oz salted butter
— 2 slices toasted sourdough
— Truffle oil to drizzle and chopped chives to garnish
— Black pepper to serve

Crack your eggs into a bowl with a pinch of salt and whisk together.

Place a frying pan over a low heat and add the butter.

Once the butter is melted and bubbling, pour in the whisked egg.

Leave to cook untouched for around 30 seconds until the edges are starting to set. Use a spatula to push the edge of the egg into the centre and then tilt the pan so the runny part runs towards the edges.

Keep repeating step 4 until the egg is almost set in a flower-like shape but the centre is still a little wet-looking.

Remove from the pan and place on top of the toasted sourdough. Drizzle with truffle oil, scatter over the chives and crack over some fresh black pepper. Eat immediately.

Truffle tartiflette V

There is nothing more comforting and special than a plate of tartiflette! It's decadent, cheesy and indulgent and I hope transports you straight to any previous mountain trips where you may have partaken of it during après ski. The addition of truffle makes it just that little bit more special.

SERVES 4

— 700g/1lb 9oz Maris Piper potatoes, peeled
— 30g/1oz butter
— 2 brown onions, finely sliced
— 2 garlic cloves, crushed
— 1 tbsp dried thyme
— 100ml/3½ fl oz crème fraiche
— 100ml/3½ fl oz double (heavy) cream
— 1 tbsp truffle oil
— 250g/9oz Gruyère cheese, grated
— Salt and pepper to season
— Sliced truffle to garnish

Start by preparing your potatoes. Set a saucepan over a high heat with a pinch of salt and bring to the boil. Chop the potatoes into slices 0.5cm/¼in thick and add to the saucepan. Boil for around 15 minutes or until tender. Drain and leave to one side.

Place a frying pan over a medium-high heat and add the butter. Once the butter is bubbling, add the sliced onion and fry till golden brown and caramelized, stirring often.

Next, add the garlic and thyme. Stir continuously and once the garlic is fragrant remove the pan from the heat.

In a bowl, mix together the crème fraiche, double (heavy) cream, truffle oil and some seasoning and set aside.

Heat the oven to 200°C/400°F and get yourself a lasagne dish.

Place half the cooked potato slices over the base of your dish. Next, add half the onion mix and half the grated cheese. Repeat with the remaining potato, onion and cheese.

Pour over the truffle cream.

Place the tartiflette in the oven for 10–15 minutes or until golden brown and bubbling. Remove from the oven and serve topped with truffle slices.

Fried chicken, waffles and gochujang sauce

This recipe is an upgrade of the American classic, with the Asian sauce making it a totally delicious fusion plate. Salty, crunchy, spicy, sticky and a little bit sweet, it's a real flavour bomb in your mouth.

SERVES 4

FOR THE FRIED CHICKEN
— 4 boneless and skinless chicken thighs
— 100ml/3floz buttermilk
— 100g/3½oz plain (all-purpose) flour
— 1 tbsp paprika
— Pinch of salt
— Vegetable oil for frying

FOR THE GOCHUJANG SAUCE
— 2 tsp sesame oil
— 1 garlic clove, crushed
— 1 tbsp fresh grated ginger
— 3 tbsp gochujang paste
— 2 tbsp soy sauce
— 2 tbsp honey
— Juice of half a lime
— Sliced spring onion and toasted sesame seeds to garnish

FOR THE WAFFLES
— 160g/5½oz plain (all-purpose) flour
— 1 tsp baking powder
— 1 egg
— 250ml/8½ fl oz/1 cup milk
— 30g/1oz finely sliced spring onions (scallions)

Start by placing the buttermilk and chicken thighs in a bowl and mixing together so the chicken is evenly coated. Leave to one side.

Whilst the chicken rests, make the gochujang sauce. Set a saucepan over a medium heat and add the sesame oil. Once the oil is hot, add the garlic and ginger, cooking for 1–2 minutes or until fragrant, stirring continuously.

Add the gochujang paste, soy sauce, honey and lime juice to the pan and mix together. Let simmer for around 5 minutes until the sauce has thickened. Remove from the heat and set aside, ready to reheat just before serving.

Next, make the waffles. Place the flour, baking powder, egg, milk and a pinch of salt in a bowl and whisk until you have a smooth batter. Stir through the spring onions (scallions).

Heat a waffle iron and add a quarter of your batter, cooking for around 6 minutes, and flipping halfway, or until golden. Repeat with remaining batter to make three more waffles and once all the waffles are cooked, keep warm in a very low oven.

Place the flour for the fried chicken along with the paprika and a pinch of salt in a bowl and mix together. Set a frying pan over a high heat with about 2cm/1in of vegetable oil.

Once the oil is hot, dip two of the buttermilk-coated chicken thighs into the spiced flour and then fry in the oil for around 8 minutes until golden brown and crispy. Transfer to a paper towel to drain off excess oil and repeat with the remaining chicken.

Warm the gochujang sauce through and then it is time to plate up.

Place a waffle on each plate and top with a crispy chicken thigh. Drizzle over the warm gochujang sauce and garnish with sliced spring onions (scallions) and toasted sesame seeds to serve.

Chipotle vegetarian quesadillas V

Cheesy, crunchy and fresh, these go down particularly well with kids and are a great way to sneak some extra veggies into them. Play around with the vegetables – they work really well with broccoli too.

SERVES 4

— Vegetable oil for frying
— 2 red onions, finely sliced
— 2 red peppers, finely diced
— 500g/1lb 2oz bite-sized cauliflower florets
— 2 tbsp chipotle paste
— 75g/2½oz cheddar cheese, grated
— 75g/2½oz mozzarella, grated
— 4 tortilla wraps
— Salt and pepper to season
— Herby avocado sauce (see page 159), salsa and coriander (cilantro) to serve

Place a frying pan over a medium heat with a drizzle of olive oil. Add the sliced onion and peppers and sauté for around 10 minutes, stirring often until soft and caramelized.

Add the cauliflower and mix together. Cook for a further 5–10 minutes until the cauliflower is tender. Stir through the chipotle paste and add some seasoning, cook for 5 more minutes and remove from the heat.

Mix together the cheddar and grated mozzarella in a bowl.

Place another frying pan over a medium heat. Add a tortilla to the pan and let toast for a minute before adding a quarter of the cauliflower mix and a quarter of the cheese.

Fold the tortilla in half and cook for 2 minutes each side until golden brown and the cheese is melted. Repeat with the remaining tortillas.

Cut the quesadillas in half and serve warm with the herby avocado sauce for dipping and coriander (cilantro) to garnish.

Dirty Shirley Temple, p139

Mortadella, burrata and hot honey sandwich

Salty, creamy, spicy and sweet – I'm not sure there is any better flavour combo! A decadent sandwich that's meant to feel like a fresher, more modern version of a brunch classic: the cheese and ham toastie. Also delicious with grilled courgettes (zucchini) added in during the summer months.

MAKES 4

— Drizzle of vegetable oil for frying
— 12 slices mortadella ham
— 4 medium ciabattas, halved
— 2 burrata balls
— Salsa verde (see page 157)
— Spicy honey

Start by crisping the mortadella. Place a frying pan over a medium heat with a drizzle of vegetable oil. Add the mortadella and fry till crispy. Remove from the heat and blot off any excess oil.

Toast the ciabatta.

Top one half of each ciabatta with half a burrata ball, a quarter of the crispy mortadella, a dollop of salsa verde and a drizzle of spicy honey.

Place the remaining ciabatta half on top and sandwich together. Tuck in!

Mimosa,
p142

Crispy chicken Caesar Benedict

Eggs Benedict has always been my standard brunch order in any restaurant and chicken Caesar my go-to salad, so I've been playing around with the perfect hybrid for years. It's rich, decadent and full of different flavours and textures, making it a real showstopper.

SERVES 4

FOR THE CAESAR SAUCE
- 80g/3oz Greek yoghurt
- 2 anchovies in oil, drained
- 1 garlic clove
- Juice of 1 lemon
- 1 tbsp Worcestershire sauce
- 30g/1oz Parmesan cheese, grated
- Salt and pepper to season

FOR THE CHICKEN
- 30g/1oz flour
- 1 egg, beaten
- 30g/1oz panko breadcrumbs
- 2 chicken breasts, halved lengthways
- Vegetable oil for frying

FOR THE BENEDICT
- 2 English muffins, halved and toasted
- 4 poached eggs (see page 156)
- Handful of cos lettuce
- Crispy onions, to garnish

Start by making the Caesar sauce. Place all the ingredients in a food processor and blitz till smooth. Season to taste and leave to one side.

Next, turn your attention to the chicken. Place the flour, egg and panko breadcrumbs in three separate bowls. Dip each chicken piece into the flour so it is properly coated, then the egg and then the breadcrumbs and place on a baking paper-lined baking tray.

Place a frying pan over a high heat with about 1cm/½in vegetable oil. Once the oil is really hot, add two chicken pieces and fry for 3–4 minutes each side till crispy and golden brown. Transfer to the tray, blot off any excess oil, season and repeat with remaining chicken pieces.

Place a toasted muffin half on each serving plate. Top with cos lettuce, a chicken piece and a couple of tablespoons of Caesar dressing. Garnish with crispy onions and serve immediately.

LAZY SUNDAY

When writing this book there was obviously a huge focus on recipes that would look beautiful for the next time you host brunch – but I felt it equally important to have a section for when hosting is the last thing you want to be doing. Enter the Lazy Sunday chapter, designed for the hungover, sleepy or 'craving something speedy' moments we all have.

This is also the page to open when you are looking for big flavour with minimum effort – think the kind of dish you would find at your local café but with a few modern twists. I imagine eating these in my pyjamas, watching a movie with a big cup of tea, and hope you make that your reality too.

Shakshuka V

A perfect recipe for having your favourite people over! Packed with vegetables, spice and protein, it feels indulgent whilst being healthy, and looks spectacular popped in the middle of the table for people to help themselves. Pair with flatbreads (see page 149) but if you don't have time to make them, toasted and buttered sourdough works equally well for mopping up.

SERVES 4

- 2 tbsp olive oil, plus extra for frying
- 2 small brown onions, finely sliced
- 3 peppers, finely sliced
- 1 tsp ground cumin
- 1 tsp smoked paprika
- ½ tsp chilli flakes (or more to taste)
- 2 tbsp tomato purée
- 2 x 400g/14oz tins of good quality chopped tomatoes
- 1 tbsp red wine vinegar
- 4 eggs
- 200ml/7oz Greek yoghurt
- 1 large garlic clove, crushed
- Juice of 1 lemon
- Pinch of salt
- 30g/1oz coriander (cilantro), roughly chopped to garnish
- Flatbreads or sourdough to serve

Place a frying pan over a medium heat with a drizzle of olive oil. Add the sliced onion and peppers and fry for 5–10 minutes until softened.

Add the cumin, paprika, chilli flakes and tomato purée and stir through. Cook for 2 minutes before adding the tinned tomatoes and red wine vinegar. Simmer for 10–15 minutes over a medium-low heat until the sauce has thickened slightly.

Make wells in the sauce and crack an egg into each. Cover and cook for 5 minutes.

Whilst the eggs cook, mix together the Greek yoghurt, 2 tbsp olive oil, crushed garlic, lemon juice and pinch of salt in a bowl and set aside.

When the eggs are cooked, garnish with coriander (cilantro) and then transfer the frying pan to the table and serve with the garlic yoghurt and flatbreads.

MAKE AHEAD

The sauce can be made in advance and stored for up to 3 days in an airtight container in the fridge until ready to use. Just place in a pan and slowly bring up to a simmer, adding a bit of water if needed to loosen, and skip to step 3.

Cheesy sausage and greens toastie

In my opinion, a sausage sandwich will always trump a bacon one, so this is a must-have brunch recipe for me. Juicy, caramelized sausage meat paired with creamy mozzarella, salsa verde for acidity and kale for a nutrient booster, all sandwiched between toasted sourdough – it really doesn't get any more comforting.

SERVES 4

- 6 pork sausages, de-skinned
- Olive oil for frying
- 100g/3½oz kale, roughly chopped
- Salted butter
- 8 pieces sourdough
- Aioli (see page 159)
- 2 balls mozzarella, thinly sliced

Alternatives

We live in a world with amazing plant-based alternatives and nowhere is that better seen than vegetarian sausages. Swap the pork for your favourite meat-free sausage to make this dish vegetarian.

Place a frying pan over a medium heat. Add the sausages and break the meat up into small pieces using the spoon. Dry fry till crispy and golden brown. Once cooked, transfer to a plate and set aside.

Place the pan back on the heat, drizzle with a little oil, add the kale and cook until wilted. Remove from heat.

Butter both sides of the sourdough pieces. Top one piece of buttered sourdough with a quarter of the sausage meat, kale, some aioli and mozzarella slices. Sandwich another slice of bread on top.

Place the frying pan back on the heat and add one toastie. Fry for 2–3 minutes each side, pushing down with a spatula throughout to help keep the toastie together.

Remove from the pan and repeat with the other three sandwiches until you have a mountain of pure deliciousness.

Masala beans on toast VE

Baked beans on toast was a typical breakfast for me as a teenager and this is the elevated version. With warming Indian spices and a little bit of heat, it makes for a perfect quick, flavoursome dish. The only trick here is to invest in good-quality baked beans for a delicious tomato sauce to make the dish all the more tasty.

SERVES 4

— Drizzle of olive oil
— 2 tsp mustard seeds
— 2 red onions, finely sliced
— 2 red chillies, finely chopped
— 2 garlic cloves, crushed
— 2 tbsp fresh ginger, grated
— 2 tsp ground cumin
— 1 tsp turmeric
— 2 tins good-quality baked beans
— Pinch of salt
— 4 slices sourdough bread, toasted
— Sliced green chilli and pickled onion to garnish

Start by placing a frying pan over a medium heat with a drizzle of olive oil. Add the mustard seeds and toast for a minute – once they start popping, add the onion.

Sauté the onion until soft and translucent. Add the chilli, garlic, ginger, cumin and turmeric. Mix everything together and gently fry for a few minutes until aromatic.

Next add the baked beans and a pinch of salt. Mix everything together and allow to simmer, stirring occasionally, for 5 minutes before removing from the heat.

Place the beans on the toasted sourdough and garnish with pickled onions and green chilli slices.

MAKE AHEAD
The beans can be made 2 days in advance and stored in an airtight container in the fridge. Simply reheat till simmering over a low heat when you want to serve.

Brunch tacos V

Tacos are a staple in my hosting line-up, so I couldn't resist creating this must-try brunch version. All the flavours you expect are wedged in a tortilla, but the real star is the herby avocado sauce. It's creamy, zesty, sweet and unusual – you won't be able to not serve it with everything once you've tried it.

SERVES 4

- 4 eggs
- 100g/3½oz cherry tomatoes, roughly chopped
- ½ red onion, finely chopped
- 30g/1oz coriander (cilantro), finely chopped
- 2 tbsp red wine vinegar
- 2 tbsp olive oil
- Pinch of salt
- 4 tortillas
- 4 tbsp herby avocado sauce (see page 159)
- 12 pickled jalapeño chilli slices

Start by soft-boiling the eggs to your taste – I prefer a yolk that's not quite runny here. Drain and run under cold water so cool enough to peel.

Next, make the tomato salsa by mixing together the chopped tomatoes, red onion, coriander (cilantro), red wine vinegar, olive oil and a pinch of salt.

Warm through the tortillas.

Carefully halve the soft-boiled eggs, ensuring you keep the yolks intact.

On individual plates, place a tortilla topped with a tablespoon of herby avocado sauce. Add a soft-boiled egg, a tablespoonful of salsa and the jalapeño chillies. Tuck in!

Alternatives

Swap the egg for roasted tofu pieces. Dice one firm block of tofu into cubes and place on a tray with a drizzle of olive oil and 2 tbsp soy sauce. Roast for 20 minutes at 200°C/400°F.

Blood orange margarita, p138

Pan con tomate with fried eggs and dukkah V

I've been lucky enough to spend a lot of time in Spain and the famous pan con tomate has always been my go-to tapas order. The key is always to invest in the best quality tomatoes you can get as the better they are, the better this dish will taste. The addition of dukkah, a Middle Eastern spice mix, gives this a Lebanese touch, and the fried egg makes it the perfect balanced brunch recipe.

SERVES 2

- 2 large good-quality tomatoes
- 1 large garlic clove
- Extra virgin olive oil
- Salt and black pepper to season
- 2 large pieces of ciabatta
- 2 eggs
- Chopped chives and dukkah to garnish

Finely grate the tomatoes and microplane the garlic into a bowl. Drizzle with some olive oil, season with salt and mix together. Leave to one side to rest.

Toast the ciabatta and place on two serving plates.

Fry the eggs until crispy on the edges but retaining a runny yolk, seasoning with black pepper as they cook.

Top each piece of bread with half the tomato mix and a fried egg. Garnish with chives, dukkah and more seasoning to taste.

Alternatives

Leave out the egg for a vegan option.

Caprese
Ham and Gruyère

Ricotta
and
blueberry
Wilted
spinach and
Parmesan
cheese

Filled croissants

Sometimes brunch might be on the go and these filled croissants (see page 88) are the perfect option. They're great to make in advance, keep wrapped in baking paper and take out for a snack whilst walking with friends. The filling options are endless but my favourite is ricotta and blueberry.

SERVES 4

— 4 croissants, cut in half lengthwise

Simply pack each croissant with your choice of filling and place in a preheated 200°C/400°F oven for around 10 minutes until the croissant is crispy and golden brown.

FILLING IDEAS
Ricotta and blueberry
Ham and Gruyère
Peanut butter and banana
Caprese – sliced mozzarella, salted tomatoes, avocado and basil
Wilted spinach and Parmesan cheese

Hash browns, trout and sour cream

A brunch classic that uses trout over salmon to make the recipe a whole lot more environmentally friendly. The hash browns make for the most delicious salty and crunchy base that lends itself to whatever brunch topping you want to play around with.

SERVES 4

- 2 Maris Piper potatoes
- ½ brown onion, finely sliced
- 1 egg
- Couple of pinches salt
- 100ml/3½ fl oz/scant ½ cup sour cream
- Juice of 1 lemon
- Vegetable oil
- 200g/7oz smoked trout slices
- Black pepper, chopped chives and lemon wedges to garnish

Grate the potatoes into a bowl with the finely sliced onion, egg and a pinch of salt. Mix everything together with your hands.

In another bowl, mix together the sour cream, lemon juice and a pinch of salt and leave to one side.

Heat a frying pan with a generous drizzle of vegetable oil. Once really hot, place a golf ball-sized piece of the potato mix into your pan and flatten down with a spatula. Flip once browned and crispy, cooking for about 3 minutes each side, and transfer to a serving plate, using kitchen paper to blot off any excess oil.

Top each hash brown with a dollop of lemon sour cream. Gently place a slice of smoked trout on top and garnish with black pepper and chives.

Serve with lemon wedges.

Alternatives

To make the dish vegetarian, replace the smoked trout slices for smoked carrot lox. Roll eight carrots in salt and lay on a roasting tray. Roast for 30 minutes at 180°C/350°F and let them cool before rubbing off excess salt. Peel the carrots into ribbons and place in a bowl with 1 tbsp maple syrup, 2 tbsp soy sauce, juice of one lemon and 2 tsp smoked paprika. Mix together and keep in the fridge overnight before using.

Soy mushroom savoury porridge VE

The first restaurant I worked in placed great emphasis on wholegrains and in particular porridge (oatmeal). It was there that I first tried savoury porridge and it's something I've been introducing to friends and family ever since. For the sceptics, think risotto but extra creamy – don't knock it till you've tried it!

SERVES 4

— 600g/1lb 5oz shitake mushrooms
— 2 tbsp soy sauce
— 1 tbsp sesame oil
— Olive oil for frying
— 2 garlic cloves, crushed
— 160g/5½oz porridge oats (oatmeal)
— 900ml/30 fl oz/4 cups vegetable stock
— 1 avocado, finely sliced
— Toasted sesame seeds and spring onion (scallions) for garnish
— Crunchy chilli oil (see page 158)

Preheat the oven to 200°C/400°F. Place the mushrooms on a baking tray and drizzle over the soy sauce and sesame oil. Mix together, spread across the tray and place in the oven. Roast for 10–15 minutes until crispy and golden brown.

Set a saucepan over a low heat with a drizzle of olive oil. Add the garlic, stirring continuously for a minute until fragrant.

Add the oats and toast for a few minutes before adding the vegetable stock and a pinch of salt. Stir often until the oats have absorbed all the stock.

Split between four bowls and top each with a quarter of the sliced avocado, a quarter of the crispy mushrooms, some sesame seeds and sliced spring onions (scallions). Top with a drizzle of chilli oil.

Brunch egg baps

A couple of years ago one of my best friends, Isobel, introduced me to the London restaurant Eggslut and, truthfully, it's become my default food delivery after a big night out ever since. Thankfully, these are also super-easy to make at home yourself and just as tasty. This sweet brioche bun with all the salty fillings is for all of you who've woken up with a self-inflicted headache.

SERVES 4

— 12 rashers bacon
— 4 eggs
— Vegetable oil for frying
— 4 brioche buns
— Brown sauce or ketchup
— 1 avocado, finely sliced
— 4 slices cheese

Lay the bacon out on a tray and place under the grill for around 4 minutes each side until crispy.

Set a frying pan over a high heat with a drizzle of vegetable oil. Once really hot, crack the eggs in and fry for around 2 minutes till the edges are crispy but yolks still runny.

Split and lightly toast the brioche buns.

Spread the bottom half of each bun with your choice of sauce and then top with avocado, bacon, a fried egg and a slice of cheese.

Sandwich together with the top bun and tuck in!

Alternatives

There are some great vegetarian bacons around now that work excellently here to make this dish vegetarian.

Crab Welsh rarebit

Coming from a family of cheese lovers, there had to be a cheese on toast recipe in here! Welsh rarebit is a cold, rainy English day classic with the addition of fresh crab making it just a little bit more special. Lavish comfort food at its best.

SERVES 2

- 30g/1oz salted butter
- 30g/1oz plain (all-purpose) flour
- 125ml/4 fl oz/½ cup strong ale
- 150g/5oz grated Gruyère cheese
- 2 tbsp Worcestershire sauce
- 1 heaped tsp Dijon mustard
- 2 large pieces sourdough
- 1 pot of 50/50 crab meat
- Juice of 1 lemon
- Handful of chopped chives
- Salt and pepper to season
- Chilli flakes and fresh herbs of your choice to garnish

Start by placing a saucepan over a medium heat. Once hot, add the butter and flour and stir continuously as you cook for 1 minute.

Add the ale and beat until you have a thick sauce, then add the grated cheese, Worcestershire sauce and mustard. Stir and when smooth it's ready.

Place your sourdough slices in an oven dish and top with the cheese sauce. Place under the grill for a few minutes until golden brown and bubbly.

Whilst the rarebit grills, quickly mix together the crab meat, lemon juice, chives and seasoning.

Place the hot Welsh rarebits on your two serving plates and top with the crab mix. Finally garnish with chilli flakes and any herbs you like and tuck in!

Alternatives

Keep it vegetarian and still just as delicious by replacing the crab with some kimchi.

Bullshot,
p143

Kedgeree

Spiced and comforting with a wonderful history, this recipe comes from a Scottish friend's mum. Always assumed to originally be an Indian recipe, story has it that it was actually created by Scottish soldiers serving in India who were missing their culinary home comforts and incorporated local ingredients to create this delicious hug-in-bowl, Anglo-Indian dream.

SERVES 4

- 400ml/14 fl oz/generous 1½ cups chicken stock
- 400g/14oz smoked haddock fillets
- 150g/5oz basmati rice
- Olive oil for frying
- 1 brown onion, finely sliced
- 1 tbsp curry powder
- 75g/2½oz frozen peas
- Juice of 1 lemon
- 20g/¾oz chopped parsley
- 4 hard-boiled eggs, quartered

Place a saucepan over a medium heat and add the stock. Bring to a simmer and add the haddock fillets, poaching for 8 minutes till just cooked.

Remove the fish from the stock, put on a plate and flake into bite-sized chunks. Add the rice to the poaching liquor and cook till all the liquid has been absorbed and the rice is cooked al dente. Remove from the heat and leave to one side.

Place a large frying pan over a medium heat with a drizzle of oil. Add the sliced onion and sauté for 5–10 minutes till soft and translucent.

Add the curry powder and mix together, gently toasting the spices.

Add the rice and peas to the pan and mix together. Stir often and cook for 2 minutes till the peas are warmed through.

Next add the flaked haddock, lemon juice and parsley. Gently mix together, being careful not to break up the haddock flakes anymore.

Split the hot kedgeree between four serving plates. Top with the egg wedges and serve. And if you like an extra dollop of flavour, add a spoon of aioli (see page 159) for a tasty kick.

Eggs and Marmite Parmesan soldiers

The grown-up version of boiled eggs and soldiers! Usually I would say keep it simple and don't over-complicate something already fantastic but the addition of Marmite and Parmesan brings so much umami you didn't even know it was missing until you try it. Another tasty alternative is to swap out the sourdough for my Anchovy and Paprika Cheese Straws (see page 152) for an extra special version!

SERVES 4

- 4 eggs
- 4 large slices of toasted sourdough
- Marmite
- 40g/1½oz Parmesan cheese, grated

Fill a saucepan with water and a pinch of salt and place over a high heat. Once the water has come to a boil, add the eggs and boil for 6 minutes for runny eggs. Drain.

Whilst the eggs cook, make the soldiers. Slice each piece of toast into 2cm/1in thick soldiers and lay on a baking tray. Spread Marmite over the top of each and scatter with some Parmesan. Place under the grill until the cheese is melted and bubbling.

Serve the soft-boiled eggs with the Marmite Parmesan soldiers for dunking.

Alternatives

Parmesan actually contains animal rennet so swap for pecorino to make this recipe vegetarian.

Bacon, egg and mango chutney naans

One of my best-loved restaurants is famous for this brunch dish so I had to include my at-home version. This is an Indian-inspired bacon and egg sandwich that elevates an English classic. Perfect for anyone craving a carby, salty and sweet hit the morning after a big night out.

SERVES 4

- 12 rashers smoked streaky bacon
- Vegetable oil for frying
- 4 eggs
- 4 mini naan breads
- 100g/3½oz Greek yoghurt
- 4 tbsp mango chutney
- 1 red chilli, finely sliced
- Handful of coriander (cilantro), roughly chopped

Lie the bacon on a baking tray and place under the grill. Cook until crispy, flipping halfway through.

Place a frying pan over a medium heat with a drizzle of vegetable oil. Crack the eggs into the pan and fry for around 2 minutes until crispy around the edges but with the yolks still runny.

Toast the naans.

Spoon a quarter of the yoghurt and a tablespoon of mango chutney onto one half of each naan. Top with three rashers of bacon and a fried egg.

Garnish with chilli slices and coriander (cilantro). Fold over and tuck in!

Alternatives

For the non-pork eaters, this works equally as well with bresola as it crisps in a similar way.

SOME-
THING
SWEET

As someone with a massive sweet tooth, this could arguably be my favourite chapter of the whole book. With everything from cinnamon buns to pistachio cake and fried crumpets, the recipes in this chapter will have your guests begging for more.

The great thing about brunch is the sweet stuff isn't something that comes at the end like a pudding, but can sit alongside the savoury dishes and be the star of the show throughout.

Chocolate crumpet bread and butter pudding V

Bread and butter pudding is an English classic many of us grew up on and love dearly. But by swapping the bread for crumpets the recipe is modernized and elevated, with the additional benefit of the crumpets having extra surface area to make more crispy caramelized parts. Perfect for brunch but equally as delicious for Sunday lunch pudding – my family go mad for this one!

SERVES 6

- 150ml/5 fl oz/½ cup double (heavy) cream
- 200ml/7 fl oz/¾ cup milk
- 75g/2½oz caster (superfine) sugar
- 60g/2oz milk chocolate
- 60g/2oz dark chocolate
- 2 eggs
- 6 crumpets
- 200g/7oz raspberries
- Toasted crushed hazelnuts, cream and chocolate shavings to garnish

Warm the cream and milk together in a small saucepan over a low heat to a simmer. Remove from the heat and add the sugar and chocolate, stirring continuously until the chocolate is melted, then set aside.

Place the eggs in a glass bowl and whisk. Add the cream mix and continuously whisk until mixed through. Set aside.

Preheat your oven to 180°C/350°F and chop the crumpets into quarters.

Tuck half the crumpet pieces into your pudding dish and scatter with half the raspberries. Top with the remaining crumpets and raspberries.

Pour over the chocolate mix and bake in the oven for 25 minutes.

Serve warm with a drizzle of cream, scattering of chopped hazelnuts and a few shavings of grated chocolate.

Pear and almond sponge with plum jam and yoghurt v

A frangipane tart is my all-time favourite pudding and this is the brunch version. The vanilla and almond sponge topped with flaked almonds and pear slices make it particularly aesthetically pleasing, so it's perfect for hosting. You can swap the fruit throughout the year, depending on what's in season, and play around with jam pairings.

SERVES 6–8

- 4 pears, peeled, cored and finely sliced
- 150g/5oz salted butter
- 150g/5oz light brown or caster (superfine) sugar
- 2 tsp vanilla paste
- 3 eggs
- 200g/7oz ground almonds
- 100g/3½oz plain (all-purpose) flour
- 1 tsp cinnamon
- Pinch of salt
- 50g/2oz toasted flaked almonds
- Plum jam, crème fraiche and thyme sprigs to garnish

Start by preheating your oven to 180°C/350°F, lining a cake or brownie tin (38 x 20cm/15 x 8in) with baking paper and prepping your pears.

Then place the butter, sugar and vanilla in a mixing bowl and whisk till really smooth and creamy.

Add the eggs, ground almonds, flour, cinnamon and pinch of salt and continue to whisk till you have a really smooth fluffy batter.

Pour the mix into your lined baking tray and smooth with a palette knife. Spread the pear slices out over the top, pressing slightly into the batter. Do the same with the flaked almonds.

Bake for 40 minutes or until cooked through and golden brown on the top. Remove from the oven and let cool.

When ready to serve, split between your plates and serve with a spoonful of crème fraiche, spoonful of jam and a scattering of thyme sprigs.

Golden syrup fried crumpet and poached rhubarb V

Last summer I had the joy of attending a supper club where I was introduced to the idea of crumpets being the base for a pudding. It led to a summer obsession of trying out so many different flavours and ingredients until I hit on this perfect combination. What I love about serving this dish is how intrigued one's guests are by it at first glance and then totally obsessed once they've bitten into it.

SERVES 6

— 400g/14oz rhubarb
— 3 tbsp maple syrup
— Juice of 1 orange
— 200ml/7 fl oz/¾ cup double (heavy) cream
— 2 tsp vanilla extract
— 50g/2oz butter
— 4 tbsp golden syrup
— 6 crumpets, toasted
— Lemon curd and chopped toasted hazelnuts to serve

Start by preheating your oven to 200°C/400°F and lining a baking tray with baking paper.

Chop the rhubarb into inch-long chunks and place on the lined baking tray, pouring over the maple syrup and orange juice. Mix together and roast for 20 minutes until the rhubarb is super-soft but still holding its shape. Leave to cool.

Whip the cream and vanilla extract in a bowl until stiff peaks form. Set aside

Next, place the butter and golden syrup in a frying pan and melt together over a medium heat. Once melted and bubbling, add the crumpets and fry for a minute each side until caramelized and all the syrup is absorbed.

When ready to plate up, place a crumpet on each serving plate. Top with some cream, a tablespoon of lemon curd and one-sixth of the soft rhubarb, and garnish with chopped hazelnuts.

Matcha
Rhubarb fizz, p140
Ricotta

Banana
Compote with seasonal fruit, p161

Banana, matcha and ricotta pancakes V

You can't write a brunch book and not have more than one pancake recipe so here are my favourite three. I love the banana version on a lazy Sunday morning, the matcha version for a special occasion, and the ricotta one for someone extra special.

MAKES 4

— 130g/4½oz plain (all-purpose) flour
— 30g/1oz caster (superfine) sugar
— 1 tsp baking powder
— Pinch of salt
— 130ml/4 fl oz/½ cup whole milk
— 1 egg
— 30g/1oz melted salted butter, plus extra for cooking

Place the flour, sugar, baking powder and pinch of salt in a bowl and mix together.

Take a jug and add the milk, egg and melted butter and whisk together.

Add the milk mixture to the flour mixture and beat till a smooth batter forms, making sure there are no lumps.

Set a frying pan over a medium heat and add teaspoon of butter. Once the butter is melted and bubbling, add a ladle of batter.

Fry for around 2 minutes until bubbles are forming on top of the surface and edges. Flip and cook for another 2 minutes until golden brown and risen. Remove from heat and repeat with remaining batter.

Serve warm, reheating in a low oven if needed.

TO MAKE THEM...

Banana – fold one mashed banana through the batter after step 3. I love serving this variety with a dollop of peanut butter, shaved chocolate and sliced banana.

Matcha – add 1 tablespoon of matcha powder to step 1. My favourite way to serve these pancakes are with a spoonful of coconut yoghurt, handful of blueberries and a drizzle of date syrup.

Ricotta – fold through 50g/2oz of ricotta after step 3. I eat these with crispy bacon, blueberries and maple syrup.

Alternatives

To make these pancakes vegan, sub the egg for a homemade chia egg. Mix 2 tbsp of chia seeds with 5 tbsp of water and let rest for 5 minutes to thicken. Replace throughout the recipe where it calls for an egg.

Brunch crumble VE

The ingredients of this nostalgic pudding lend themselves so nicely to a brunch recipe, with fruit and oats playing the starring roles. Paired alongside cold soy yoghurt for a perfect contrast, the buttery caramel, crispy crumble topping is so delicious! I think this recipe is wonderful served hot, warm or cold.

SERVES 10

— 400g/14oz cooking apples
— 30g/1oz vegan butter
— 200g/7oz blackberries
— 2 tsp cinnamon
— 3 tbsp maple syrup
— Cold soy yoghurt to serve

TOPPING
— 200g/7oz porridge oats
— 100g/3½oz vegan butter, softened
— 100g/3½oz demerara sugar
— Pinch of salt

MAKE AHEAD
The crumble can be made up to step 6 ahead of time. Cover with cling film (plastic wrap) and store in the fridge for up to 2 days before using.

Start by peeling, coring and chopping the apples into 1cm/½in cubes.

Place a large saucepan over a medium heat and add 30g/1oz of vegan butter. Once bubbling, add the apples and sauté for 10 minutes, stirring often until the apple has softened.

Add the blackberries, half the cinnamon, the maple syrup and 3 tbsp of water. Mix together and let simmer for around 15 minutes till the sauce has thickened.

Whilst the compote cooks, make the crumble topping. Place the oats, 100g/3½oz vegan butter, demerara sugar, remaining cinnamon and a pinch of salt in a bowl and mix together.

Preheat the oven to 200°C/400°F.

Pour the compote into an ovenproof dish and top with the crumble. Place in the oven for 20 minutes until the top is caramelized and compote bubbling.

Remove from the oven and let rest for 5 minutes before serving with a big spoonful of soy yoghurt.

Blackberry shrub, p135

Lemon, pistachio and ricotta cake v

Over the years I have cooked for many gluten-free clients and, after much testing, this is the sponge recipe I will now always use. In fact, I love this cake recipe so much it's become my default for every friend's birthday. The pistachio makes the sponge the most vibrant green and is moist and decadent against the lemony, fluffy ricotta.

SERVES 10–12

- 225g/8oz pistachios, blitzed till ground almond texture
- 50g/2oz ground almonds
- 225g/8oz caster (superfine) sugar
- 2 tsp baking powder
- Zest of 2 lemons for cake
- Juice of 1 lemon for icing
- Pinch of salt
- 6 eggs
- 260ml/9 fl oz/1 cup olive oil
- 150ml/5 fl oz/generous ½ cup double (heavy) cream
- 250g/9oz ricotta
- 4 tbsp icing sugar
- Crushed chunky pistachio and grated chocolate to garnish

Line a cake tin with baking paper and oil the sides. Preheat the oven to 180°C/350°F.

Place the ground pistachios, almonds, sugar, baking powder, lemon zest and pinch of salt in a bowl and mix together.

Add the eggs and olive oil to the dry ingredients and mix together until you have a smooth batter.

Pour into the tin and bake for an hour or until a knife comes out clean. Once cooked, leave to cool in the tin for 10 minutes before removing and letting cool completely on a wire rack.

Whilst the cake bakes, make the icing. Beat together the double (heavy) cream, ricotta, lemon juice and icing sugar until a thick consistency. Store in the fridge until ready to use.

Once ready to serve, top the cake with the icing and garnish with pistachio chunks and grated chocolate. Serve and store any leftovers in the fridge for up to 2 days.

Cinnamon buns v

A cinnamon bun from my local bakery is a post-gym Saturday morning tradition that survived my entire twenties – and one I hope to carry with me for life. There is no better way to start a day than with something sweet, soft, crunchy and laced with cinnamon, so why not make this something we share with friends too.

MAKES 12

— 200ml/7 fl oz/¾ cup whole milk
— 100g/3½oz salted butter for the dough, plus 75g/2½oz for filling
— 500g/1lb 2oz strong bread flour
— 1 x 7g/¼oz pack fast-action yeast
— 2 tsp ground cinnamon for dough plus 2 tbsp for filling
— 40g/1½oz caster (superfine) sugar for dough and 100g/3½oz for filling
— Pinch of salt
— 2 eggs, beaten, for the dough, plus 1 for brushing

TOPPING
— 120g/4oz icing sugar
— 1 tsp vanilla extract
— 60g/2oz cream cheese

Warm the milk and 100g/3½oz of butter in a saucepan over a medium heat until the butter is melted. Remove from the heat and leave to cool till lukewarm.

Next, place the flour, yeast, 2 tsp of cinnamon, 40g/1½oz caster (superfine) sugar and a pinch of salt into a large mixing bowl. Mix together and then create a well in the centre.

Add the warm milk mixture and two eggs. Stir everything together until a sticky dough is formed.

Gently flour a surface and turn out the dough. Knead for 5–10 minutes until the dough is smooth and less sticky. Shape into a large round and place into a lightly greased bowl.

Cover with a tea towel and leave to prove (proof) for around an hour in a warm place until doubled in size.

While the dough proves, make the filling. Place the remaining butter, cinnamon and caster sugar in a bowl and beat together until it forms a smooth spreadable consistency. Set aside.

RECIPE CONTINUES OVERLEAF

Chocolate smoothie, p143

Cinnamon buns continued

Once the dough has risen, turn out on to a lightly floured surface.

Roll out into a rectangle shape until the dough is about 1cm/½in thick. Spread the filling mix out over the dough carefully.

Roll the dough into a roulade shape and cut into 12 pieces. Place on a lined baking tray, cover with a tea towel and leave to prove for a further 40 minutes until risen.

Brush the tops of each bun with beaten egg and bake in a preheated 200°C/400°F oven for 10–12 minutes or until golden brown. Remove and let cool.

Whilst the buns cook and cool, make the topping by mixing together the icing sugar, vanilla extract and cream cheese in a bowl till a smooth icing consistency.

Once the buns are completely cooled, spread the icing on top and serve!

Chocolate banana bread V

During lockdown we were all making banana bread and this is my favourite version after months of recipe testing. I wanted to create something that was just as delicious as any café version but slightly lighter. The combination of spelt flour, ground almonds and Greek yoghurt make for a super-light and fluffy sponge you won't be able to get enough of.

MAKES ONE 1lb LOAF

- 175g/6oz white spelt flour
- 100g/3½oz ground almonds
- 2 tsp bicarbonate of soda
- 1 tsp vanilla extract
- 100g/3½oz Greek yoghurt
- 2 eggs
- 125ml/4 fl oz/½ cup olive oil
- 125ml/4 fl oz/½ cup maple syrup
- Pinch of salt
- 3 very ripe bananas, mashed
- 200g/7oz dark chocolate (70%), broken into small chunks

Preheat your oven to 180°C/350°F and line a 500g/1lb loaf tin with baking paper.

Place the flour, ground almonds, bicarbonate of soda, vanilla extract, Greek yoghurt, eggs, olive oil, maple syrup and pinch of salt in a bowl. Whisk together to a smooth batter – I always use an electric whisk for speed.

Fold through the mashed banana and chocolate chunks and spoon into your lined loaf tin.

Bake for 50 minutes or till a skewer inserted comes out clean. If the top starts to burn, cover with tin foil for the last 10 minutes.

Enjoy warm or cold – it's also delicious with yoghurt and seasonal berries.

Sticky toffee banana pudding V

Sticky toffee pudding will forever be my ultimate comfort food dish so I had to get a variation of it in the book somewhere. With the addition of a banana bread sponge paired alongside the thick Greek yoghurt, this might be my favourite recipe in the whole book.

SERVES 8–10

- 150g/5oz pitted dates
- 1 tsp bicarbonate of soda
- 150g/5oz salted butter, plus 100g/4oz for sauce
- 150g/5oz dark muscovado sugar, plus 150g/5oz for sauce
- 1 tsp vanilla extract
- 150g/5oz plain (all-purpose) flour
- 1 tsp baking powder
- 3 eggs
- 2 pinches of salt
- 3 ripe bananas, mashed
- 100ml/3½ fl oz double (heavy) cream
- Thick Greek yoghurt, to serve

Preheat oven to 180°C/350°F and line a 38 x 20cm (15 x 8in) brownie tin with baking paper.

Roughly chop the dates into bite-sized pieces. Place in a bowl with the bicarbonate of soda and 150ml/5 fl oz/½ cup boiling water. Mix together and leave to rest whilst you make the batter.

Place the butter, muscovado sugar, vanilla extract, flour, baking powder, eggs and a pinch of salt in a mixing bowl. Whisk until a smooth, light batter forms. Add the dates, with their liquid, and the mashed banana to the batter and fold through.

Pour the batter into the lined brownie tin. Place in the oven and bake for around 40 minutes until cooked through.

While the sponge cooks, make the sauce. Warm the remaining butter and sugar in a saucepan over a medium heat. Stir continuously until the butter is melted and the sugar dissolved.

Let thicken slightly before removing from the heat, then add the cream to the pan and stir quickly to make a delicious thick toffee sauce. Add a pinch of salt and stir through.

Serve the sponge warm, cut into squares and topped with a dollop of Greek yoghurt and a drizzle of the salty toffee sauce.

Affogato,
p128

Chocolate babka V

Originating from Jewish communities in Ukraine and Poland, babka is a braided brioche loaf that was originally filled with jam or cinnamon before chocolate became more widely available. It's half cake, half bread and a real labour of love that's worth all the extra effort.

SERVES 8

— 100ml/3½ fl oz/scant ½ cup whole milk
— 40g/1½oz butter
— 300g/10½oz strong bread flour
— 1 x 7g/¼oz packet fast-action yeast
— 75g/2½oz caster (superfine) sugar, plus 75g/2½oz for syrup
— Pinch of salt
— 1 egg, beaten
— 2 tsp vanilla extract
— 150g/5oz hazelnut chocolate spread
— Crushed pistachios to garnish

Place the milk and butter in a saucepan over a medium heat, stirring often until the butter has melted in with the milk. Remove from the heat and let cool until lukewarm.

Next, place the flour, yeast, sugar and a pinch of salt in a large mixing bowl. Mix together and create a well in the centre.

Pour in the milk mixture, egg and vanilla extract. Mix together until a sticky dough forms.

Turn out the mixture onto a lightly floured surface and knead for 5–10 minutes until a smooth elastic ball forms and the dough is springy to pressure. Put in a greased bowl and set in a warm place covered with a tea towel for around an hour until the dough has doubled in size.

Once the dough has risen, turn it out onto a lightly floured surface and roll into a rectangle about 1cm/½in thick.

Spread the hazelnut chocolate spread over the dough gently, leaving a little space around the edges.

Roll the babka into a roulade shape with the seam on the bottom. Cut in half lengthwise.

Chocolate babka continued

With the cut side facing up, place one piece on top of each other to form an X. Twist the pieces of dough around each other and tuck the ends underneath. Place in a greased 500g/1lb loaf tin, cover with a tea towel and let prove (proof) for around an hour in a warm place until risen.

Bake in a preheated 180°C/350°F oven for 30 minutes until golden brown.

Whilst the babka bakes, make the syrup by placing the remaining sugar and 75ml/5 tbsp water in a saucepan over a medium heat. Bring to the boil and once the sugar has dissolved, remove from the heat.

Once the babka is cooked but still hot, brush with the syrup and scatter over the pistachios. Let cool in the tin before serving.

Affogato V

SERVES 4

- 4 large scoops of really good quality vanilla ice cream
- 4 double shots of hot espresso
- Amaretto (optional)
- Crushed pistachios and chocolate shavings to garnish

A more shake-like version of the famous Italian pudding. This recipe really feels like the epitome of the fusion of breakfast and lunch to me, with breakfast's coffee and lunch's ice cream pudding combined – two things that would never work the other way around.

Place each vanilla ice cream scoop in a low tumbler.

Pour a shot of hot espresso over each scoop and drizzle with amaretto, if using.

Garnish with some crushed pistachios and chocolate shavings and serve.

Maple, cinnamon and nut granola VE

When hosting, there's nothing I love more than a recipe that can be made well ahead of time but still be loved as much as one you spent hours stressing over. This very low-effort recipe is one I think you'll make time and time again, as not only is it very addictive to eat, it's also just great to always have around as your guests will love it. I like to serve it with Greek yoghurt and my fruit compote (see page 161).

MAKES 10–12 PORTIONS

— 270g/9½oz porridge oats (oatmeal)
— 100g/3½oz nuts of choice
— 100g/3½oz seeds of choice
— 1 tbsp ground cinnamon
— Pinch of salt
— 120ml/4 fl oz/½ cup olive oil
— 120ml/4 fl oz/½ cup maple syrup
— 100g/3½oz raisins

Preheat the oven to 180°C/350°F.

Place the oats (oatmeal), nuts, seeds, cinnamon and a pinch of salt in a roasting pan and mix together.

Add the olive oil and maple syrup to the roasting pan and stir everything together so the oats are evenly coated. Spread the mix out over the pan and place in the oven for 30–45 minutes, stirring a few times until it's golden brown and crispy.

Remove from the oven and let cool completely before stirring through the raisins. Store in an airtight container.

Sumac roasted strawberries and whipped mascarpone French toast V

Many of us have nostalgic memories of the way we ate French toast as kids. For me, it was in summer with chopped strawberries, a drizzle of cream and lashings of maple syrup. Whilst that still sounds absolutely delicious, I wanted to make a more grown-up version with the addition of vanilla, sumac and mascarpone.

SERVES 4

- 250g/9oz mascarpone
- 100ml/3½ fl oz double (heavy) cream
- 120g/4oz icing sugar
- Zest and juice of 1 lemon
- 2 tsp vanilla extract
- 400g/14oz strawberries, hulled and halved
- 1 tbsp sumac
- Pinch of salt
- 100ml/3½ fl oz milk
- 4 eggs
- 1 tbsp ground cinnamon
- 50g/2oz butter
- 4 thick slices of brioche bread

Start by preheating your oven to 200°C/400°F.

Place the mascarpone, double (heavy) cream, half the icing sugar, the lemon zest and 1 tsp of the vanilla extract in a bowl and whisk till lightly whipped. Store in the fridge until ready to use.

Now place the strawberries, sumac, remaining vanilla extract, remaining icing sugar, lemon juice and a pinch of salt on a lined baking tray and mix together. Roast for 20 minutes, mixing halfway through, until soft and sticky. Leave to cool to room temperature.

Next, whisk together the milk, eggs and cinnamon in a shallow bowl. Then set a frying pan over a medium heat and add half the butter. Let it start to bubble and melt.

Next dip two of the brioche slices into the egg mix for around 30 seconds to let it soak up some of the liquid. Place in the hot frying pan and fry for 2 minutes each side until golden brown and caramelized.

Remove from the heat and repeat with the remaining brioche.

Split between four serving plates and top with a dollop of whipped mascarpone. Then spoon over the roasted sumac strawberries and their juices and serve!

DRINKS

Some would argue that the drinks are more important than the food, but whatever the answer I certainly know that they are very important and something not to be forgotten when hosting your next brunch.

Whether it be a simple Bellini, a brunch classic like the Bloody Mary or a chocolate smoothie, this chapter has you totally covered and gives you enough fun drink recipes to really wow your guests, whatever the occasion.

Dad's Bloody Mary

Never did I think my dad would ever have his own recipe feature in a cookbook as he is famously awful in the kitchen, but here we are! Many Sundays growing up were spent drinking the Virgin Mary version of his recipe with a packet of salty crisps and I'm yet to try one as good. He says that plenty of fresh lemon juice is the real key ingredient.

SERVES 4

- 1.2 litres/2½ pints good quality tomato juice (I love any with clam juice added)
- Juice of 1–2 lemons
- 2 tsp horseradish
- 1 tbsp Worcestershire sauce
- 1 tsp celery salt
- Couple of drops of Tabasco (to your spice levels)
- 100ml/3½ fl oz vodka (optional)
- 50ml /2 fl oz sherry (optional)
- 4 celery sticks

Pour the tomato juice into a large jug and add the lemon juice, horseradish, Worcestershire sauce, celery salt and Tabasco.

Mix together and season to taste – remember, Dad thinks the key is lemon juice!

If adding, mix through your spirits to make it a Bloody Mary.

Pour into ice-filled glasses, add a celery stick to each and serve.

Blackberry shrub

I was first introduced to shrubs whilst spending a month working in a tiny kitchen one particularly hot English summer and I've yet to find anything that quenches your thirst more. Best described as a grown-up cordial with vinegary undertones, it is delicious served with plenty of ice.

SERVES 4

— 200ml/7fl oz white wine vinegar
— 225g/8oz caster (superfine) sugar
— 225g/8oz blackberries

Place the vinegar and sugar in a small saucepan over a medium heat. Bring the mix to the boil and stir until the sugar has dissolved.

Tip the blackberries into a 1 litre/2 pint jar and pour over the hot vinegar mix.

Use a fork to mix and crush the blackberries and vinegar mix together. Place the lid on the jar and store in a cupboard for 4 days to ferment.

Line a fine sieve with a clean muslin cloth and pour through the shrub mixture into another clean jar. Store in the fridge for up to two weeks and use as and when you like with the vinegar flavour mellowing over time.

When serving, mix a double shot of the shrub with 200ml/7 fl oz of soda water and serve over ice with a rosemary sprig and a few fresh blackberries. Add a shot of vodka or gin to turn it into a cocktail.

Pineapple paloma, p139

Blackberry shrub, p135

Dirty Shirley Temple, p139

Grapefruit and rosemary Moscow Mule

Grapefruit and rosemary is one of my favourite flavour pairings and it works so well here with the ginger beer. It's aromatic, super-fresh and the perfect palate-cleanser – you will make this again and again!

SERVES 4

— Juice of 3 grapefruits
— Juice of 2 limes
— 400ml/14 fl oz ginger beer
— 4 sprigs rosemary
— 200ml/7 fl oz vodka (optional)

Pour the grapefruit juice, lime juice and ginger beer into a jug and mix together. If adding the vodka, stir through now.

Fill four tumbler glasses with ice and add a rosemary sprig to each.

Split the Moscow mule mixture between each glass and serve.

Blood orange margarita

Margaritas are really having their moment and while the original lime one makes the perfect supper drink pairing, changing them here for blood orange gives this cocktail a slightly sweeter taste and more brunch feel.

SERVES 4

— 200ml/7 fl oz freshly squeezed blood orange juice
— Juice of 2 limes
— 200ml/7 fl oz tequila
— 100ml/3½ fl oz triple sec
— 1 tsp caster (superfine) sugar
— 1 tsp sea salt
— Pinch of hot chilli powder
— 4 blood orange slices

Pour the blood orange juice, lime juice, tequila and triple sec into a jug and stir together. Cover and store in the fridge until ready to serve.

When ready, mix together the sugar, salt and chilli powder on a plate. Run a blood orange slice over the rim of your margarita glasses and then dip each one into the chilli salt mix.

Fill the glasses with crushed ice and a blood orange slice each.

Split the margarita mix between the four glasses and serve.

Pineapple paloma

The addition of pineapple to this recipe instantly transports you somewhere hot and sunny, making it the perfect drink pairing to so many of the Mexican-inspired dishes in this book.

SERVES 4

— 400ml/14fl oz fresh pineapple juice
— Juice of 3 limes
— 200ml/7 fl oz tequila
— 400ml/14 fl oz tonic water
— 4 lime wedges

Pour the pineapple juice, lime juice, tequila and tonic water into a jug and stir together.

Fill four tumblers with ice and a lime wedge each and pour in the paloma mix.

Dirty Shirley Temple

Taking a childhood favourite and making it a lot more grown up! This is a proper thirst-quencher filled with nostalgia.

SERVES 4

— 200ml/7 fl oz vodka
— Juice of 4 limes
— 120ml/4 fl oz grenadine
— 500ml/17 fl oz soda water
— Lime wedges to serve

Fill four tall glasses with ice.

Place the vodka, lime juice, grenadine and soda water into a jug and mix together.

Pour into the ice-filled glasses, add a straw, top with a lime wedge and serve.

Rhubarb fizz

Pretty, pink and absolutely delicious – nothing better for a girls' brunch! Make the rhubarb syrup fresh during spring when rhubarb is in season or get your hands on some really good-quality premade stuff.

SERVES 4

— 120ml/4 fl oz gin
— Juice of 2 lemons
— 40ml/1½ fl oz rhubarb syrup
— Prosecco to top up

Pour the gin, lemon juice and rhubarb syrup into a cocktail shaker filled with ice and shake to mix together.

Split between four champagne flutes, top with prosecco and serve.

Bellini

A brunch classic that never gets old! Originally from Venice, this drink will transport you straight to a hot summer's day in Italy.

SERVES 4

— 3 peaches
— Champagne, prosecco or lemonade
— Mint sprigs to garnish

Peel the peaches, remove the stone and place in a food processor. Blend till smooth before splitting between four chilled champagne flutes

Top each glass with your chosen fizz, mix together and garnish each with a sprig of mint.

Rhubarb fizz, p140

Mimosa

One for summer when the oranges are particularly sweet and delicious. Replace the champagne or prosecco with lemonade to make a non-alcoholic version.

SERVES 4

— 400ml/14 fl oz freshly squeezed orange juice
— 400ml/14 fl oz champagne or prosecco
— Juice of 1 lime

Place all the ingredients into a jug, mix together and serve in champagne flutes with a little ice.

Green juice

Fresh, zingy and delicious, a real vitamin- and nutrient-booster for when you are craving something a little healthy. Play around with this recipe as little or much as you like. I love to sub the apples for pears for a fun flavour twist.

SERVES 4

— 100ml/3½oz spinach
— 2 apples, cored and chopped into wedges
— 3cm/1in piece fresh ginger
— 30g/1oz mint
— Juice of 1 lemon

Place the spinach, apple, ginger and mint in a juicer.

Once all the ingredients are blitzed, add the lemon juice.

Best served cold or with ice.

Bullshot

Best served outside to warm you up when it's cold but sunny – no drink feels more apt on a winter's day.

SERVES 4

— 400ml/14 fl oz beef consommé
— 200ml/7 fl oz vodka
— 1 tbsp Worcestershire sauce
— Juice of 1 lemon
— Tabasco, to taste
— Black pepper

Place the beef consommé in a saucepan over a medium heat. Bring to a simmer and remove from the heat.

Pour the hot consommé into a jug with the vodka, Worcestershire sauce, lemon juice, Tabasco and plenty of cracked black pepper.

Serve hot, warm or cold.

Chocolate smoothie

It doesn't get much better than a chocolate flavoured smoothie that's actually good for you. This one is thick, creamy, sweet and extremely addictive.

SERVES 4

— 4 sliced frozen bananas
— 4 heaped tbsp peanut butter
— 4 large medjool dates, pitted
— 4 tbsp cacao powder
— 900ml/30 fl oz almond milk
— Pinch of salt

Put all the ingredients in a food processor and blitz until smooth.

Season to taste with more dates for sweetness, peanut butter for nuttiness or cacao for a more chocolatey flavour. If you prefer a thicker smoothie, add a few handfuls of ice and blitz till smooth.

SIDES, SAUCES AND EXTRA BITS

For me, a chef is only as good as their repertoire of sauces, so I've brought you some of my all-time favourites. They elevate a meal, hide any mistakes and bring in even more exciting flavour.

You will also find some extra side bits here that are great on the go or just to bulk up a menu. Some feature as recommended sides in previous recipes, but there are also a couple, like the garlic king prawns, that I just couldn't not share with you.

Cheesy jalapeño cornbread v

Hugely popular in the US, this is a dish I think we don't make enough of across the pond. Traditionally, it sits somewhere between a cake and bread that's a little sweet, thanks to the corn, but is made spicy and salty here with the addition of jalapeños and cheese.

MAKES 16 SQUARES

— 150g/5oz plain (all-purpose) flour
— 150g/5oz fine polenta
— 2 tsp baking powder
— 50g/2oz sugar
— Pinch of salt
— 225ml/8 fl oz/scant 1 cup whole milk
— 1 egg
— 75g/2½oz salted butter, melted
— 165g/6oz tinned sweetcorn, drained
— 100g/3½oz cheddar cheese, grated
— 30g/1oz jalapeño chillies, finely sliced

Preheat the oven to 180°C/350°F and line a brownie tin (38 x 20cm/15 x 8in) with baking paper.

Place the flour, polenta, baking powder, sugar and a pinch of salt in a mixing bowl and stir to combine.

Add the milk, egg and melted butter to the bowl and beat together until a smooth batter.

Next add the sweetcorn, cheddar cheese and sliced jalapeños. Fold through so the jalapeños and sweetcorn are evenly distributed throughout the batter.

Pour the batter into the lined brownie tin and place in the oven to bake for 20 minutes or until a skewer inserted comes out clean and the top is golden brown.

Let cool slightly in the tin before removing and cutting into squares and serving warm. Also delicious served cold!

Porridge bread V

I've been making loaves of this recipe for years and always have so much fun playing around and mixing up the flavour variations. It's so easy to make, protein-rich, and I'm not sure anything can beat it toasted and slathered with salted butter and raspberry jam. Don't be afraid to mix up the seeds, nuts and dried fruits to suit what you like or simply use up any open packets you have in the pantry.

MAKES 1 LOAF

- 300g/10½oz porridge oats (oatmeal)
- 500g/18oz Greek yoghurt
- 2 eggs
- 1 tbsp bicarbonate of soda
- 50g/2oz pistachios, roughly chopped
- 50g/2oz pumpkin seeds
- 50g/2oz raisins
- Pinch of salt

Line a large 1kg/2lb loaf tin with baking paper and preheat the oven to 180°C/350°F.

Place all the ingredients and a big pinch of salt into a mixing bowl. Stir everything together so properly combined and the nuts, seeds and raisins are evenly distributed.

Pour the batter into the lined tin and bake for 45 minutes or until a skewer inserted comes out clean.

Remove from the oven and let cool completely before turning out from the tin.

Serve cold or toasted.

Easy flatbreads V

This is the kind of the recipe that you won't be able to stop making after you've realized how easy and delicious it is! The perfect mopper, scooper and base – and I recommend you play around with different spice flavours.

MAKES 4

— 200g/7oz plain (all-purpose) flour
— 200g/7oz Greek yoghurt
— 1 tsp baking powder
— Pinch of salt
— 1 tbsp cumin seeds
— 50g/2oz salt butter
— Drizzle of vegetable oil

Put the flour, yoghurt, baking powder and pinch of salt in a bowl and mix together with your hands.

Once it's all sticking together, transfer to a lightly floured surface and knead for around 2 minutes until a smooth dough is formed. Place back in the bowl and let rest for 5 minutes.

Tip the cumin seeds in a frying pan over a low heat and gently toast. Once fragrant, add the butter, melt and leave to one side.

Divide the dough into four balls and flatten each with the palm of your hand to about 1cm/½in thick.

Set a frying pan over a medium-high heat and gently drizzle with vegetable oil.

Add two of the flatbreads and cook for 1–2 minutes each side till puffed up, golden brown and crispy. Remove from the heat and repeat with the remaining dough.

Brush the flatbreads with the cumin butter and serve.

Crispy smashed potatoes VE

Crunchy, herby, salty, sweet and sticky – no more words needed!

SERVES 4

— 500g/1lb 2oz baby potatoes
— Salt and pepper to season
— Rapeseed (canola) oil for baking
— 30g/1oz chopped mixed hard herbs (I like rosemary, thyme and sage)
— Drizzle of honey (optional)
— Pinch of sea salt

Start by preheating the oven to 200°C/400°F, then place the potatoes in a saucepan and cover with water. Add a pinch of salt, set on the heat and bring to the boil.

Once simmering, cook for 10 minutes or until the potatoes are tender throughout. Drain and leave cooling in the sieve for 5 minutes.

Line a baking tray and tip the potatoes out on the tray.

Using an old glass jam jar, lightly press down on each potato to flatten them a little but not so they lose their shape.

Drizzle with rapeseed (canola) oil and season. Place in the oven and roast for around 30 minutes until golden brown and super crispy.

Remove from the oven and immediately add the chopped herbs to the tray. Mix them in with the potatoes, letting the herbs cook a little in the residual heat.

Serve immediately with a drizzle of honey, if using, and a pinch of flaky sea salt.

Potato rosti V

Salty, crunchy and just the best base for anything savoury!

MAKES 12

- 750g/1lb 10oz Maris Piper potatoes
- 1 small brown onion, finely sliced
- 1 tbsp plain (all-purpose) flour
- ½ tsp baking powder
- 1 tbsp dried thyme
- 2 eggs
- Vegetable oil for frying
- Salt and pepper to season

Peel and grate the potatoes. Place in a clean tea towel and ring out any excess water.

Place the grated potato, onion, flour, baking powder, thyme and eggs in a mixing bowl and beat together until they become a well-combined and smooth batter. Season.

Set a large frying pan over a medium-high heat with a generous drizzle of vegetable oil.

Spoon half the batter, separating into four rostis, straight into the hot pan and flatten into round palm-sized shapes. Fry for 3–4 minutes each side until crispy and golden brown.

Once cooked, transfer to a plate lined with kitchen paper to remove any excess oil and repeat steps 3 and 4 with the remaining batter.

Eat immediately or reheat in the oven for 10 minutes when ready to serve.

Anchovy and paprika cheese straws

You might be thinking I'm a little mad including a cheese straw recipe in a brunch book, but bear with me until you've tried this recipe and dunked them in a soft-boiled egg. I'm yet to try a combo more filled with umami and saltiness than this and I think it's a joy you all need to experience.

MAKES 16 STRAWS

- 1 pre-rolled sheet of puff pastry, room temperature
- 45g/3oz anchovy fillets, crushed to a paste in a pestle and mortar
- 50g/2oz grated Parmesan cheese
- 1 tsp paprika
- 1 egg, beaten

Preheat the oven to 200°C/400°F and line two baking trays with baking paper.

Roll out your puff pastry sheet and spread the anchovy paste over the whole sheet.

Cut the pastry sheet widthways into strips 2cm/1in thick.

Scatter the Parmesan out evenly across the strips and sprinkle over the paprika.

Pick up one strip and carefully twist into a cheese straw shape and place on your baking tray. Repeat with the remaining strips to fill both trays.

Brush lightly over the strips with the beaten egg.

Place in the oven and cook for 15 minutes until the pastry is puffed, golden brown and crispy. Enjoy warm or cold!

Spring onion and pancetta egg muffins

One for when you are on the move or simply trying to add a bit more protein to the table. These can be made ahead of time so are a great weekday breakfast or mid-morning snack.

MAKES 12

— 100g/3½oz cubed pancetta
— 1 red pepper, finely diced
— 6 eggs
— 30ml/1 fl oz milk
— 1 pack of spring onions (scallions), finely sliced
— 50g/2oz grated Parmesan cheese
— 1 tsp chilli flakes, optional
— Salt and pepper to season
— Oil or butter for greasing

Preheat the oven to 180°C/350°F and lightly grease each muffin hole of a 12-hole muffin tray.

Set a frying pan over a medium heat and add the pancetta. Dry fry for 5 minutes until starting to crisp and then add the peppers. Sauté for 2 minutes to slightly soften the peppers. Remove from the heat.

Place the eggs, milk and a pinch of salt in a jug and whisk together. Add the pancetta mix, spring onions (scallions), grated cheese, chilli flakes (if using) and some seasoning, and stir together.

Pour the muffin mix evenly into all the greased muffin holes.

Place in the oven and bake for 15 minutes or until cooked throughout and golden brown.

Let cool slightly in the tin before removing and enjoying warm or cold.

Garlic king prawns

Seafood is something we need to see more of at brunch, and prawns (shrimp) in particular. Not only are they delicious and high in protein, they are really fast to cook and low effort, but still have that special feel. Serve with some delicious bread and, if you want to make it extra special, add a dollop of paprika hollandaise on top (see page 158).

SERVES 4

— 75g/2½oz butter
— 3 garlic cloves, crushed
— 16 large king prawns (jumbo shrimp), de-shelled and cleaned
— 30g/1oz parsley, roughly chopped
— Juice of 1 lemon
— Salt and pepper to season

Place a frying pan over a medium-high heat and add the butter.

Once the butter has melted, add the garlic. Stir continuously and cook for around a minute till the garlic is fragrant.

Next, add the prawns (shrimp) and cook for 5 minutes, stirring often, till pink and cooked through.

Remove the pan from the heat and add the parsley, lemon juice and seasoning.

Transfer to a serving plate and serve hot.

Perfectly poached eggs

A good poached egg is a thing of beauty and not as tricky to make as many people think. Use my tried and tested method for a perfect poaching, and for an extra-special classic brunch touch, pair your eggs with some homemade hollandaise sauce (see page 158).

Fill a large saucepan with water, place over a high heat and bring to the boil.

Add 1 tbsp of white wine vinegar and lower the heat so the water is at a gentle simmer.

Crack the egg into a fine strainer and let the runny egg white run off before placing in a small bowl.

Stir the water to create a gentle whirlpool, carefully slide the egg into the water and let cook for 3–4 minutes until the white is cooked through.

Remove from the heat with a slotted spoon onto a kitchen paper-lined plate to blot off any excess water.

Chimichurri

- 50g/2oz parsley
- 50g/2oz coriander (cilantro)
- 1 garlic clove, grated
- 1 tbsp dried oregano
- 1–2 tsp chilli flakes
- 45ml/1½ fl oz red wine vinegar
- 100ml/3½ fl oz extra virgin olive oil
- Salt and pepper to season

Finely chop the parsley and coriander (cilantro) and place in a jar.

Add the garlic, oregano, chilli flakes, red wine vinegar, olive oil and seasoning.

Whisk together till emulsified and season further to taste. Store in the fridge for up to 3 days until ready to use.

Salsa verde

- 50g/2oz parsley
- 30g/1oz basil
- 2 tbsp capers
- 2 anchovy fillets
- 1 garlic clove, grated
- 1 tbsp Dijon mustard
- Juice of 2 lemons
- 100ml/3½ fl oz extra virgin olive oil
- Salt and pepper to season

Finely chop the parsley, basil, capers and anchovy fillets and place in a lidded jar.

Add the garlic, Dijon mustard, lemon juice, olive oil and seasoning.

Whisk together till emulsified and season further to taste. Store in the fridge for up to 3 days until ready to use.

Crunchy chilli oil VE

— 2 garlic cloves, crushed
— 40g/1½oz fried crispy onions
— 1 tbsp miso paste
— 1 tbsp chilli powder
— 100ml/3½ fl oz extra virgin olive oil
— 50ml/2 fl oz sesame oil
— 2 tsp chilli flakes
— Pinch of salt

Prepare your ingredients and then place them all in a jar.

Whisk together and store in an airtight jar.

Hollandaise, with flavour variations V

— 3 egg yolks
— 1 tbsp Dijon mustard
— 1 tsp white wine vinegar
— Salt and pepper to season
— 200g/7oz salted butter
— Juice of 1 lemon

Place the egg yolks, mustard, white wine vinegar and some seasoning in a glass bowl and whisk together. Fill a saucepan with an inch of water and bring to a gentle simmer.

Melt the butter in a second saucepan over a medium heat. Once melted, remove from the heat.

Continuously whisk the egg mix as you gently drip in the hot melted butter.

Now, place the glass bowl on top of the simmering water pan and continue to whisk as the sauce thickens over the heat.

Once it's a thick yoghurt consistency, remove from the heat and whisk through the lemon juice. Serve immediately or store for up to 3 days in the fridge for later use.

VARIATIONS
Stir through 30g/1oz chopped chives for a subtle onion flavour or a pinch of paprika for a smoked flavour once you have removed your hollandaise from the heat.

Aioli, with flavour variation V

- 3 egg yolks
- 2 tbsp Dijon mustard
- Juice of 1 lemon
- 2 garlic cloves, grated
- Salt and pepper to season
- 425ml/14 fl oz rapeseed (canola) or other neutral flavoured oil
- White wine vinegar, if required

Place the egg yolks, Dijon mustard, lemon juice, garlic cloves and seasoning in a bowl. Use an electric whisk to mix together.

Keeping the whisk on, start adding the oil, drip by drip, until it is all incorporated and you have a thick garlic mayonnaise. If too thick, add a tablespoon of white wine vinegar to loosen.

Store in the fridge for up to 7 days in an airtight container.

VARIATIONS
For a herby aioli, blitz 30g/1oz each of basil, parsley, chives, tarragon and 2 tbsp of olive oil together in a food processor till smooth. Fold through the aioli once it's ready.

For a spicy aioli, fold through 2–3 tbsp of sriracha, depending on how spicy you like it, at the end.

Herby avocado sauce V

- 50g/2oz coriander (cilantro)
- 50g/2oz parsley
- 1 avocado
- 120g/4oz Greek yoghurt
- 3 tbsp honey
- 1 green chilli
- 1 tbsp apple cider vinegar

Place all the ingredients into a food processor with a pinch of salt and blitz until smooth.

This can be served immediately or stored in the fridge for up to 3 days.

Compote with seasonal fruit VE

- 450g/1lb seasonal fruit (for example, apple in winter, rhubarb in spring, berries in summer and blackberries in autumn)
- 3 tbsp honey or maple syrup
- Pinch of salt

Depending on the choice of fruit, cut into bite-sized pieces if applicable.

Place the fruit, honey or maple syrup, 3 tbsp water and salt in saucepan over a medium heat. Stir often and bring to a boil.

Once simmering, bring the heat down low and let bubble away for around 10 minutes till the sauce has thickened.

When cooled, the compote can be stored in the fridge for up to 3 days.

MENU PLANS

The whole time I was writing this book, I had a vision of all the recipes being served alongside each other in different ways to create all sorts of different brunch hosting experiences. Whether it's the perfect menu and table to be eaten in the garden on a hot sunny day, something a little more refined, or a group of recipes that transport your table to an entirely different part of the world, I hope this section has got it covered.

Alongside the menus, I thought it just as important to include some tablescaping tips to help you commit to the theme even further and create a table to support the delicious menu. I think the really fun part of creating a theme is that it makes the whole experience for your guest a little bit more exciting because it's a bit different, so why not go all out with the table, too!

Each menu includes sweet and savoury recipes with a drink pairing. They are designed to feed six but I have also added suggestions on how to scale the recipes up or down so you don't have too much or too little for the number of guests. Use the recipe log on pages 16–17 to find the recipes.

I hope you find this part of the book a real help as you become the king or queen of hosting brunch going forward!

Summer al Fresco

This menu was designed to be eaten over a long period of time as you and your guests bask in the sun, so I suggest splitting it into two courses with the pistachio cake being served later on like a pudding. With the first course, I suggest having all the plates down the centre of the table with the flatbreads dotted around in different baskets so they are in reach of everyone who wants more of them to use as vehicles for scooping.

THE TABLE

Take inspiration here from picnics with a red or brown gingham tablecloth topped with matching napkins. Use plenty of rattan on the table in the form of bud vases, napkin rings or placemats, and make the most of any vintage mismatched crockery you may have. This one is meant to be about an effortless but charming feel, so pick flowers from the garden or get your hands on some summery dahlias, sunflowers or lilies from the supermarket that can be placed in bud vases with lots of foliage to bulk them up.

Suggested dishes for six people

1 x Slow-cooked courgettes, salted yoghurt and zaatar
2 x Tomato butter beans, salsa verde and anchovy
1 x Whipped ricotta with crispy sage and burnt butter
2 x Easy flatbreads
1 x Lemon, pistachio and ricotta cake
2 x Blackberry shrub

MAKE IT FOR FOUR

Keep the courgettes and ricotta quantities the same but only make a single portion of the tomato butter beans. Scale down the shrub and easy flatbreads as per the recipe.

MAKE IT FOR TEN

Double the courgette and whipped ricotta recipe, but keep the tomato butter beans the same. Make two of the cakes, and three of the flatbreads and shrub recipes.

Mexican fiesta

Mexican might be my favourite cuisine of all time, so the idea of a fiesta menu plan was something I had in mind the entire time I was writing this book – because this is the menu I want to make the most myself! It's punchy, full of flavours and spice and a real visual showstopper that your guests will love. Serve it all up together on a side table, buffet style, so can people can keep going up and helping themselves as much as they like.

THE TABLE

I love the idea of this table being all about the notion that nothing is too much, and having all the colour you could ever want. Start with a rainbow-woven table runner, bring out all the colourful glassware, go wild on the flowers and use your most out-there serveware.

Suggested dishes for six people

2 x Huevos rancheros
2 x Trout ceviche and crispy rice
1 x Fried eggs, miso dressing and charred corn salad
1 x Jalapeño cornbread
2 x Pineapple paloma

MAKE IT FOR FOUR

Only have one serving of huevos rancheros and trout ceviche, remove the corn salad and have one quantity of pineapple paloma according to the recipe.

MAKE IT FOR TEN

Double the corn salad recipe, make another serving of the trout and scale up the pineapple paloma quantities.

Comfort food

This will no doubt be the menu you lean on the most for 6 months of the year and I think it will truly bring you so much happiness again and again. It's carb heavy, indulgent, got just enough zing and flavour to balance it all out, and has a perfect combination of salty meat and fish set against fresh seasonal vegetables.

For me, the drink is its own course here! I imagine this Bloody Mary being given to your guests as soon as they walk in ready for them to stand and chats before sitting down. Once everyone is in their seats, ask them to come up and help themselves to all the savoury options. Let people have seconds and clear away before putting the showstopper crumpet pudding right in the middle of the table for people to help themselves.

THE TABLE
Taking inspiration from all the autumnal colours, I love the canvas to start with an orange, brown or green patterned tablecloth topped with brown rattan placemats, plenty of warming dinner candles in different height holders, with real acorns and foliage weaved throughout the table. Add more layers with lots of fabrics and textures: velvet napkin rings, table lamps with patterned shades and green cabbage serveware.

Suggested dishes for six people

1 x Sausage and rosemary hash
1 x Aioli (herby)
1 x Hash browns, trout and sour cream
1 x Caramelized squash with chive, pistachio and ricotta pesto
1 x Chocolate crumpet bread and butter pudding
1 x Dad's Bloody Mary

MAKE IT FOR FOUR
Keep the quanities the same but remove the hash browns to make the menu a little lighter.

MAKE IT FOR TEN
Double of the hash browns, sausage hash and squash recipes and scale up the Bloody Mary mix.

Mediterranean style

The big party menu! This one includes some of my favourite recipes from the book and, truthfully, every time I read it, it makes me hungry. It's a menu full of colour, flavours and textures and is designed to leave your guests' jaws dropping at the number of dishes that keep coming out. I imagine this being served in courses but, in true rule-bending brunch style, the sweet comes first here.

I love the idea of guests sitting down to a pre-made bowl of yoghurt with the granola and compote as a fruity starter, accompanied with a glass of the Moscow mule. Once everyone has finished their granola bowls, let the invasion of small plates to the table begin!

THE TABLE

Start with a striped tablecloth (I'd go for a green one) and cover the table with bud vases filled with sunflowers – nothing feels more Mediterranean than big yellow sunflowers. Think ruffled stripy napkins in a different colour, real lemons scattered round the table, green or blue candle holders and glassware, and big jugs of water with lemon slices and rosemary sprigs.

Suggested dishes for six people

1 x Compote with seasonal fruit
1 x Maple, cinnamon and nut granola
1 x quantity of Grapefruit and rosemary Moscow Mule
1 x Garlic king prawns
1 x Honey and sesame halloumi with beetroot yoghurt
1 x Burrata, prosciutto and charred peach
1 x Roasted asparagus, crispy beans and romesco
1 x Crispy smashed potatoes

MAKE IT FOR FOUR

Still making 1 serving of everything but remove the crispy smashed potatoes as these are a filler that you won't need with fewer people.

MAKE IT FOR TEN

Double of the prawns, halloumi, burrata, asparagus and potato recipes and scale up the Moscow mules as per the recipe.

Fusion feast

A selection in homage to the many weekends I've spent researching brunch recipes at restaurants – where my fork would jump from my savoury plate to the sweet one at every other mouthful. For this smaller menu, I picture all of the dishes being eaten at the same time, so the Asia-inspired ingredients can complement each other.

THE TABLE

I like the idea of this being served with no tablecloth against a bare table as the recipes are so colourful and exciting on their own you don't want your guests to be distracted. If you did want to add a bit of colour, this might be time to get out any colourful solid placemats, plenty of tea lights and use white crockery to act as a blank canvas to all the colour and coloured glassware.

Suggested dishes for six people

6 x Soy mushroom savoury porridge
6 x Matcha pancakes
2 x Pineapple paloma

MAKE IT FOR FOUR

Simply scale down the porridge and pancakes to four quantities of each and keep the same quantity of paloma.

MAKE IT FOR TEN

Double the porridge and pancakes quantities and scale up the paloma mix as you like.

Continental brunch

A sweet and salty heaven! Carbs, cheese, chocolate and coffee are the main standouts with this menu and I think your guests are going to be pretty happy to sit down and enjoy this combination. I imagine this brunch being hosted in a slightly shambolic, Alice in Wonderland-themed kids' party kind of way, with all the food being eaten by hand, kids on sugar highs and parents nursing affogatos.

THE TABLE

Best served with a Provence-inspired tablescape that exudes simple elegance! A blue printed tablecloth topped with bud vases filled with lavender and foraged greenery, mix-matched serveware and cutlery, simple linen napkins and lots of added textures with rattan placemats and different sized glasses. The more clutter the better – butter dishes, bread baskets, salt and pepper shakers, etc.

Suggested dishes for six people

1 x Mortadella, burrata and hot honey sandwich
1 x Cheesy sausage and greens toastie
1 x Cinnamon buns
1 x Chocolate banana bread
2 x Affogato

MAKE IT FOR FOUR

Only make one of the sandwich recipes and choose between the buns and banana bread. Scale down the affogato.

MAKE IT FOR TEN

Double the serving of both sandwich recipes and scale up the affogato.

Closing Remarks

There is nothing more enriching than being around those we love, surrounded by good food! I really hope the recipes in this book can play a small part in your special moments with your favourite people, whether it be simply introducing you to a new easy brunch recipe to enjoy on a lazy Sunday or making you into the new brunch host extraordinaire. It has been such a life-long dream to write a cookbook and I really hope this is one you will have forever and go back to again and again.

I also hope that you might be inspired to use these recipes, as well as the get ahead and hosting tips, at other meal times, such as lunch and dinner. Even the tablescaping suggestions from the menu plans can be repurposed for other occasions and celebrations – just as brunch has no limits, I really hope you find the recipes in this book have none, too.

I hope you are as excited to start hosting brunch for friends as I am for you, and that this book gives you the confidence, tools and inspiration to send out the save the dates to your guests and to get started on a very exciting new hosting chapter.

Georgia

About the Author

GEORGIA HEARN is a private chef, supper club host and content creator. A graduate of Leiths School of Food and Wine, she now runs her own catering business which focuses on entertaining. She has worked with brands including Oliver Bonas, BBC Good Food and LuxGen. Find her on Instagram @georgiahearn__

Index

D

E

F

G

H

Text copyright © Georgia Hearn 2026
Photography copyright © Danielle Wood 2026

1

Commissioning editor: Lucy Carroll
Art Director: James Empringham
Production Controller: Marion Storz
Photographer: Danielle Wood
Food stylist: Jessica McIntosh
Prop stylist: Max Robinson

Cataloguing in Publication Data is available from the British Library

ISBN 9781035429707

Printed and bound in China by C&C Offset Printing Co., Ltd.

Headline's policy is to use papers that are natural, renewable and recyclable products and made from wood grown in well-managed forests and other controlled sources. The logging and manufacturing processes are expected to conform to the environmental regulations of the country of origin.

HEADLINE PUBLISHING GROUP LIMITED
An Hachette UK Company
Carmelite House
50 Victoria Embankment
London EC4Y 0DZ

www.headline.co.uk
www.hachette.co.uk

The authorised representative in the EEA is Hachette Ireland, 8 Castlecourt Centre, Dublin 15, D15 XTP3, Ireland (email: info@hbgi.ie)